Calling on the Prophets

Endorsements

If you care enough to be serious about the tragedy of millions of Muslims who have never had a friendly discussion with a Christian which whet his or her appetite to hear more …

If you deeply desire to be God's instrument to become a forever friend of a Muslim who truly wants to please Allah but doubts that s/he ever can … then, you will want to take the time to soak up Colin's fresh new book *Calling on the Prophets*. It delightfully illustrates how to utilize the Old Testament Prophets to open Muslim hearts, creating a desire in them to "bow the knee" to the Lord Jesus, Isa Al Masih. Highly recommended!

Rev. Dr. Greg Livingstone
founder, Frontiers

This is exactly what the mission world needs today—a practitioner sharing his inside experience and wisdom. Colin is both personable and practical, making this an extremely valuable resource for those wishing to share their Christian faith with Muslims.

Roland Muller
author of *Honor and Shame* and *The Messenger, The Message and The Community*

Colin Bearup writes from extensive firsthand experience of sharing his faith with Muslims. He demonstrates how we too can do this in a simple way that does not cause unnecessary offence and is, in fact, attractive to many Muslim listeners. In *Calling on the Prophets* you will learn about the Islamic understanding of our biblical prophets and also gain a better understanding of those prophets from a Christian viewpoint. More importantly, you will learn how you can use this understanding of the prophets to share your faith. By doing so, you will be following the example of the first apostles. While citing the prophets is not the key that unlocks every door, it is a wonderful thing to have in your toolbox.

Brother CW
The Mahabba Network, London

When talking to your Muslim friend, have you ever quoted Paul when you easily could have quoted Psalms of David? Motivated by a deep love for Muslims, Colin Bearup reminds us again and again that it is not *truth spoken* that matters, but *truth understood.* And by looking at the prophets, Colin helps us see how we can do better in getting our Muslim friends' attention and helping them understand the message God wants them to hear. The result is a treasure box of sound and immensely practical advice. A great book, and highly recommended! Get it, read it, and learn from it!

Jonathan Gutkecht
WEC International

Calling on the Prophets has given me many new insights into understanding the prophets and how to vehicle the truth of the gospel through using their life stories and deeds in a meaningful and accurate way with Muslims. Colin Bearup stresses that love for Muslims is the priority. Our aim should be to have good relationships and to be able to speak truth understandably into the lives of the people around us. The stories of prophets such as Abraham, Joseph, and Jesus are very useful for opening a discussion and reading some verses from the Bible with our Muslim friends. Colin uses many good practical suggestions and examples to help us to be better prepared to meet those seeking and needing the Truth—the Lord Jesus. I am very thankful for this valuable new resource. As a North African, this treasure helps me to display the truth to Muslims in a loving way without getting sidetracked into trying to win arguments. I highly recommend this helpful piece of work.

Brother Ben Hamou

This is one of the best books on evangelizing Muslims that I have read in my life. Not only did I read it, but I put it into practice right away. This is a relevant book for anyone who wants to share the gospel with Muslims without first becoming an expert on Islam. It serves as a bridge from what Muslims already know to what is essential—and thus to discover the plan of salvation in Jesus for their lives. At the same time, *Calling on the Prophets* awakens in us the awareness of our responsibility to share the good news of reconciliation with Jesus Christ. I am grateful to benefit from Colin Bearup's in-depth personal reflection and his effective experiences of interacting with Muslims.

François Iraguha
church planter among the Fula people in West Africa

Calling on the Prophets

In Christian Witness to Muslims

COLIN BEARUP

Calling on the Prophets: In Christian Witness to Muslims

Published by William Carey Publishing
10 W. Dry Creek Cir
Littleton, CO 80120 | www.missionbooks.org

William Carey Publishing is a ministry of Frontier Ventures
Pasadena, CA 91104 | www.frontierventures.org

Cover and Interior Designer: Mike Riester
Cover image: J Lee, unsplash.com
Copyeditor: Andy Sloan
Managing Editor: Melissa Hicks

ISBNs: 978-1-64508-391-7 (paperback)
978-1-64508-393-1 (mobi)
978-1-64508-394-8 (epub)

Printed Worldwide

25 24 23 22 21 1 2 3 4 5 IN

Library of Congress Control Number: 2021937820

All the prophets testify about him
that everyone who believes in him
receives forgiveness of sins through his name.
Acts 10:43

Contents

Preface

When I was looking for people to review and commend this book to others, I particularly wanted to hear from practitioners—from people who week in and week out are actively sharing the gospel with Muslim friends and neighbours. Mission thinkers, strategists, and theologians all have their place, but I wanted to hear from those who are wrestling daily with how to communicate faithfully and effectively with real people. This book is intended first and foremost for such as them.

I was amazed and humbled by the responses I received. "Brother CW" is working in the hyper-diverse environment of London among Muslims from all over the world. Jonathan is German and oversees work in the Arab world. I needed to know that this book would be accessible to those, like Jonathan, for whom English is not their first language. François is African, from Rwanda. We live in a time in which African Christians are taking up the challenges of world mission, and François is in a pioneer setting in West Africa. Brother Ben is himself North African, of Muslim parentage, and has been engaged in face-to-face mission in three very different contexts.

Two of these reviewers spoke of the book containing treasure. What a great image that is! The idea of "treasure" conjures images of gems. The jeweler does not create the beauty or majesty of a precious stone, but rather cuts, polishes, and sets it in such a way that its beauty is brought to light. Pastors present the prophets in one way to bring out one kind of truth; theologians may display them in another away. This book is about reaching into the treasure chest of the Bible and drawing out gems, and then polishing them and setting them in such a way that Muslims see the truth about Jesus.

The first four chapters outline the principles upon which this approach is based and discuss the reasoning behind it. The subsequent ten chapters apply the principles to specific Bible characters known to Muslims as prophets. None of this is intended to replace approaches that anyone else is using, but rather to offer a supplement, an extra resource. The task of sharing the good news with Muslims is not as simple as we often imagine before we set out. *Calling on the Prophets* is not intended to offer a set of messages or studies to memorise so much as to introduce a new skill that you can learn to use and integrate into what you are already doing.

It is my hope and prayer that many will use the material presented here to enrich their witness and that many more Muslim people will be drawn to Jesus when they glimpse the treasure that he brings.

Acknowledgments

This book would never have been completed without the input and encouragement of several people. I would particularly like to thank Dave Stockwell, who gave very constructive feedback at an early stage in the project. It was also helpful to have input from Jan Pike, who has been developing similar material in her work with women.

Richard Priestley and Chas Woods kindly read the manuscript and encouraged me along the way. My colleague Jonathan Gutknecht reviewed the manuscript; I very much appreciate his contribution, not only in the light of his experience but also from his point of view as a non-native English-speaker.

Finally, my thanks to my long-suffering wife, Jean, a faithful critic and patient proofreader!

Chapter 1 The Local Cleric

I was melting. I had walked a couple of miles in the intense African afternoon sun. This was in a city, not the desert, and the waves of oven-like heat radiated off the road surface. I was in N'Djamena, the capital of Chad. The object of my outing was to visit Saleem, a young Arab man of my acquaintance, a solid but not overzealous Muslim. When I got to the house, I met his father standing in the entrance. He told me that Saleem had gone abroad to study. I said I was pleased for him and to send him my greetings. I was going to leave, but Saleem's father had other ideas. He told me that Saleem had said I might come, and he insisted on welcoming me in. He sat me in an airless room, and other family members crowded in. The heat was much the same as it had been outside, but now without the breeze. My clothes rapidly became drenched with sweat. Like I said—melting.

The members of the family were only entertaining me to be polite. I made small talk and drank Coca-Cola, increasingly aware of the big wet patch I was making on their armchair. When my Coke bottle was empty, I felt I had fulfilled my obligations and got up to leave. But as I was getting up, I almost collided with a young man carrying a tray of hot, sweet tea. So I resumed my place. Having consumed the required two glasses, my confidence that I could politely leave was rising.

Just then, an older man burst into the room. He declared in no uncertain terms that Islam was the only true religion and that all non-Muslims were lost. He sat down opposite me, fixed his eyes upon me, and asked, "Who are you?"

He was a local Muslim cleric. Not an academic or an expert, just the local no-nonsense man. I told him I was a teacher of the Holy Books: the *Tawraat* of Moses, the *Zaboor* of David, and the *Injeel* of Jesus. All eyes turned on the cleric. "Yes," he said, "the *Tawraat* is good." He then launched into a discourse about Abraham the great Muslim. I let him run on. I was, after all, on his turf.

After a while I cut in by saying, "And don't forget Abraham is called *Khaleel Allah*." That is Abraham's Islamic title, and it means the "Friend of God."

He stopped and eyed me curiously. "How do you know that?" he asked.

"It's in the Scriptures," I replied.

Having seized the initiative, I continued. "Isn't it extraordinary that any mere man could ever be called a friend of God, for God is our mighty Creator who knows all things, sees all things, and needs nothing. How was Abraham able to become the friend of God? Only by the grace of God. Nothing Abraham could ever do would earn him the right to be God's friend. Abraham believed God and God reckoned him righteous, and so he became the friend of God. How is it that everyone knows that Abraham was the friend of God, but no one asks this question: Doesn't God intend anyone else to become his friend, as Abraham did?"

The imam looked thoughtful for a moment, and then resumed his preaching. As he went along, he mentioned the name of Joseph. Muslims know Joseph primarily as the prophet who was nearly seduced by a wicked woman. But much of the rest of his story—his rejection by his brothers, his time as a slave and then as a prisoner, and his ultimate elevation to chief minister—is also in the Qur'an in Sura (chapter) 12.

In the last few years, a number of movies have been made about Joseph's life. Although Muslims know parts of his story, they rarely consider its full implications. What indignities Joseph suffered before he was elevated! They routinely deny that God permits his prophets to suffer public shame and disgrace, and that therefore he could not possibly have allowed Jesus to suffer the shame of the cross.

A second time I spoke up. "Sir, what do you think of Joseph's suffering? How bitter it must have been to be rejected and sold by his own brothers? If his own brothers betrayed him, who was left to rescue him? And the shame of it! A rich young man suddenly finds himself made the slave of pagan foreigners. He was falsely accused. He was thrown into prison, even though he was a righteous man, and languished there for more than two years. How could God let him suffer?"

"But God delivered him," said the cleric.

"Yes, praise God. Almighty God raised him up from being the imprisoned slave to the powerful chief minister. And as chief minister he was able to save his brothers from the famine. So, we see that God has given us a sign. It was God's will that Joseph should suffer and then be exalted, all to save his unworthy brothers."

"Truly God is great," replied the imam.

I felt that I had taken him as far as I could in one session. It was finally time for me to leave. I tentatively offered him a New Testament. He practically snatched it from my hand. The family members remained present, polite, and unmoved.

Spiritual hunger had surfaced in one person I met that day, the one who seemed at first to be the most aggressive and the least open. What opened the door was making appropriate references to the prophets of God.

When I tell this story in churches, people are very impressed with my knowledge of Arabic and of Islam. The truth is, you don't have to speak Arabic—the vast majority of Muslims don't—and on our own soil they do us the favour of learning our language. As to knowing about Islam, you don't have to become a great scholar to do what I was doing.

This book is intended to get you started.

Chapter 2 Why Read This Book?

George was the only Christian working in a supermarket in a British city. A good number of the staff were Muslims of Pakistani origin. One day, one of these Muslims spoke to George. "You are not like the other white people," she said. "You worship God. You and I are the same."

George's answer came quickly. "We are not the same. My God died for me. Your God did not die for you, did he? We are not the same."

She did not approach George again. He had given her an answer which made no sense to her. More than that, his answer communicated rejection. George was genuinely pleased with his answer and with her response. His desire not to be thought of as "like a Muslim" was much stronger than his desire to communicate the good news. He was quite correct in saying that they were not the same. She was approachable and friendly. He was not.

That is a true story, if a little extreme! As Christians, we do have good news for all people, Muslims included. More than that, we have the privilege and joy of being the ones whom God intends to speak through. If you feel inclined to think God could have chosen someone more suitable than yourself, you are probably right. I think that of myself all the time. In the end, however, that is God's problem, not ours. Our job is to believe it and to follow his leadings and promptings. In Christ, we are the light of the world (Matt 5:14). That, of course, has huge significance for how we live, not just what we say. In George's case, his faith in God was noticed, but when the opportunity came, he had neither the right words nor the right attitude. What should he have said?

The material in this book focuses on what we say and how we say it. How we speak is, and always will be, secondary. In other words, unless we live as light, our words will have no power to do good. To paraphrase 1 Corinthians 13:1, unless we love Muslims, our talk is just a noise. But if we are looking to God to help us love them as we should, and if we are trusting his Holy Spirit to enable and empower us, then it is entirely appropriate to apply ourselves to gain a little know-how, and that is where this book comes in.

Hidden Obstacles

When it comes to communicating the good news to Muslims, several obstacles that Christians aren't even aware of need to be overcome. To start with, many Muslims don't expect Christians to have anything to offer. At best, they regard Christians as second-rate Muslims. After all, they are taught that Islam came about to correct and complete the religions that had gone before. Even a faithful member of an older religion must be lacking something that is to be found in the new one. Muslims are taught to regard Jesus Christ as a prophet of Islam whose message has been misunderstood and distorted by his followers.

The mere fact of our being Christians makes us an unreliable source of truth. Furthermore, for the Muslim on the street a Christian is simply someone who was born into a Christian country. On countless occasions in the UK, I have heard Muslim individuals casually refer to their white British neighbours or work colleagues as "Christians." But when they look closely, they see people who don't know the first thing about God. Many Muslims are themselves pretty lax about religious matters, but were they to get serious, why should they expect to learn anything useful from "those Christians"? This is just one reason why godliness of character is so important.

Furthermore, Muslims don't know that they are "lost." That term is not in their vocabulary. Nor do they know that salvation exists, so why would they seek it? Salvation in the biblical sense simply isn't a feature of Islam. By and large, Muslims aren't trying to "earn salvation through works." That is just our evangelical perception of them. According to Islamic teaching, God created humankind to be weak. People need religion to guide them. God gives religion. Humanity's job is to submit. The very name "Islam" is the Arabic word for submission.

Consequently, most Muslims assume that Christianity works essentially the same way; that is, we have to submit to our religion—end of story. They can't imagine that any Muslim would have anything to gain before God by changing from one religion to another. When they hear of someone converting to Christianity, they assume it must be for money or for other worldly advantage. What other reason could there possibly be?

Very Basic Principles

In order to help our Muslim friends, we need to get their attention; and then once we have their attention, we need to hold their interest. First and foremost comes how we live, especially that we love and respect them. Then we need to express truth in such a way that it interests our Muslim friends, stimulates questions, and opens up possibilities.

It is actually quite easy to say things that are *true*, but *not interesting*. George, for example, said something that was true, but incomprehensible. For his Muslim workmate, there was only one God, so why speak of two? And what sense does it make to say that any god could or would die?

Here is a more subtle point. Almost any statement that begins with "We believe" seems to be a statement *not about truth*, but *about Christians*. We do this all the time without realising it. Furthermore, the term *Christian*, for a Muslim, is an exclusive category. The Christians are *someone else*. There is no reason why something that *Christians* believe—even good Christians—should be relevant to them, except perhaps as general knowledge. It carries no incentive to learn more.

A subject of conversation becomes interesting when it is surprising, intriguing, and relevant. For example, if a Muslim assumes, as many do, that all "Christians" have given up on religion, then our bringing God into the conversation creates a point of interest. Talking about God's love and concern for all people (not just for that ambiguous word *us*) is a good starting point.

Similarly, my experience indicates that many Muslims have the impression that Christians are only interested in Jesus, whereas they see themselves as faithful to all the prophets. Indeed, many prophets are mentioned in the Qur'an, and the message they bring always matches that of Muhammad. Therefore, it makes perfect sense to them to say that they believe in all the prophets and that they feel no reason to actually read the Bible. Consequently, our bringing other prophets into the conversation may arouse the curiosity of spiritually alert Muslims. It's not that all Muslims are the same, but bringing the prophets into the conversation creates possibilities that many will respond to in one way or another.

In addition to saying something that is true and interesting, we want to say something that is useful. Many Muslims will quite happily talk with us about the evils in the world or how ineffective the legal system is or how far astray youth culture is going, but what they need to hear is the good news. From my perspective, something is *useful* when it takes them a step closer to understanding who Jesus Christ is, what he has done for them, and why they need him. It is quite possible to talk about religion with Muslims without ever making progress along that particular path. Jesus came to give them new life, and it is a tragedy if our Muslim friends never even begin to perceive that.

My aim in this book is quite narrowly defined. There are already a lot of excellent books that explain what Islam is and explain the basic dos and don'ts of presenting Christ to Muslim people. My intent is to address a subject which, to the best of my knowledge, no other book covers: namely, how to share the good news of Jesus by making use of the prophets of whom Muslims have heard and whom they respect. I see this book as an addition to all the good material that is already available.

The Lie of the Land

Whenever we speak to a Muslim about God, what we say will come under one of three headings: common ground, disputed ground, or neutral ground. We need to be aware of these categories and of when we are moving from one to another. It is not that some areas are off-limits, but we need to be thinking about what it takes to get through each kind of terrain. We can stroll casually down a country path, but we would pick our way very carefully through a minefield. Knowing which is which is, to put it mildly, very useful.

The common ground consists of those things on which we all agree, which is actually quite a lot. Many Christians have a tendency to be impatient to get out of the common ground and into disputed areas, but if we want to build good relationships and gain a listening ear, we should use the common ground to the full.

What precisely is the common ground? Examples include that there is only one God, that Moses was a prophet, that the world we live in belongs to the Creator, and that everyone must give account of their lives to God. The disputed ground consists of the areas of sharp disagreement. These are well known and concern some very important matters, such as Jesus being the Son of God and dying on the cross.

The map of disputed ground has been drawn for us; the lines are historic and well defined. We need to remember that if we blunder carelessly into one of these disputed areas and our friend is offended or upset, their reaction is not about their personal opinions or convictions. They are only responding according to their upbringing. As those who have good news to communicate and a commitment to love our neighbour, we are the ones responsible to find ways of navigating the disputed ground with our friends for their good.

What is less apparent to many is the existence of a vast swathe of neutral ground, which consists of true information about God and the ways of God that are unfamiliar to Muslims. There is plenty to choose from, but what is useful is information which helps them understand the good news without setting off their defences. To get a hearing, our message needs to be interesting. Key subjects include the promises of God, the plan of God, and the lives of the prophets.

The approach used in this book is to use the common and neutral ground to the maximum. It isn't possible to bring someone to Christ without passing through the disputed ground as well, but we only enter it carefully, intentionally, and wisely.

And Finally: A Hint

Most Christians have a narrow view of salvation and how it works. They understand it the way their own church presents it. The Bible uses a wide variety of terms when speaking of salvation, but we tend to filter them according to our own culture and tradition. In Scripture, the lost are found, light has come to those in darkness, the separated are reconciled, and so on. The book of Hebrews speaks of salvation in terms of purification.

When we go cross-cultural, we need to be ready to broaden our understanding. This is not a compromise nor a deviation from the truth. The gospel is rich and deep, and there are many aspects of it that we rarely encounter within our own culture. People raised in a different culture will never see things exactly as we see them, nor should they. We too are perceiving the truth through our own cultural filters. To help people with a different cultural background, we need to access the diversity of the gospel. Our objective shouldn't be to get others to see God's Word from exactly the same angle we do, but rather that they engage with God's Word and receive it from *their* own angle. As we do this, our understanding will be enriched and we will broaden our own view of what the Bible is about. If you find that the material in this book looks at familiar prophets in unfamiliar ways, now you know why.

Chapter 3 Who Are the Prophets?

Although Muslims and Christians acknowledge many of the same prophets, we have major differences of understanding.

Seven Things We Need to Know about Prophets in Islam

1. All the Prophets Were Muslims

Many Christians are surprised at the idea that all the prophets were Muslims. We regard Islam as a religion founded in seventh-century Arabia. However, Islam describes itself differently. According to Islamic teaching, it is the one and only true religion that there ever has been or ever will be. For example, one verse in the Qur'an, 7:172, says:

> And when Your Lord summoned the descendants of Adam, and made them testify about themselves. "Am I not your Lord?" They said, "Yes, we testify." Thus you cannot say on the Day of Resurrection, "We were unaware of this."[1]

This is taken to mean that at the beginning of creation, God called together all the people that would ever be descended from Adam and required them to testify that they knew of God and had no excuse for not worshipping him.

1 ClearQuran translation available from www.quranful.com.

What we call "Islam" today is only its most recent and complete form. Technically, *Islam* means "submission to God." To put it another way, Islam means obedience to the one true creator God. Therefore, every obedient believer from the creation of the world was a Muslim. Since there is only one God, there can only be one religion. All the prophets, as faithful believers who obediently brought messages from God, were not only Muslims but good examples to all Muslims. See, for example, Q 2:135–136 and 6:83–87. This view is perfectly coherent. It is just different from ours.

This is how Islam is taught. That doesn't mean that every Muslim understands it this way. Many are untaught and many confuse their ethnicity or their nationality with their religion. Christians have been known to do the same thing. Nevertheless, the idea that all the prophets were Muslims is deeply rooted and is reflected, for example, in naming practices. Children are named Yusuf (Joseph) and Ibrahim (Abraham) because they are understood to be inherently Muslim.

2. The Prophets Are Sent to Peoples

The Qur'an teaches that God sent at least one prophet to every people (Q 16:36; 35:24). Some prophets were believed by those to whom they were sent; others were not. They all preached essentially the same message—namely, that only one God exists and that people should worship him alone, rejecting all idols. Each of the earlier prophets had at least part of the revelation, but Muhammad brings the complete revelation. The details of how that worship was to be expressed varied from place to place and from time to time, because God can do as pleases him. Judaism is seen as a religion that developed from the Islam that was handed down to Moses. Christianity likewise arose from the Islam handed down through the prophet Jesus.

The differences of practice are accounted for either by God's inscrutable will or by the human tendency of turning from the ways of God. This view of things means that there is no awareness of biblical prophetic history. The fact that God sent many prophets to just one people, the Jews, to prepare the way for a global Saviour comes as a total surprise to many Muslims. The Qur'anic picture is rather of many prophets at different times all with essentially the same unchanging message. Although Muslims know the names of many of the prophets found in the Bible, we shouldn't expect them to have any idea of the order the prophets came in or of the unfolding of a divine plan.

3. Each Prophet Has His Time

One universally held view of prophethood is that later prophets replace earlier prophets. What God has most recently said overrides anything that came before.

This is fundamental to Islamic thinking and it is what cements Muhammad into place. It is not a matter of one contradicting another or any dramatic changes of direction, rather that the most recent is the most authoritative. This idea is so taken for granted that our Muslim friends probably assume that we hold the same view. It would therefore come as a surprise that we accept the authority of many prophets and that we hold that these prophets complement each other.

Although Muslims think of the prophets as succeeding one another, they rarely have any awareness of prophetic chronology. A moment's thought will show why that would be. Since Muhammad has replaced all the others and since the Qur'an is seen as the full and complete revelation, what value is there in looking into the lives and times of previous prophets? They have all been replaced. If you have the latest computer, why would you want to go back to a Windows 95 machine? The Qur'an, along with its supporting traditions (the *Hadeeth* literature), recounts the stories of past prophets only to illustrate and express its own message. As a result, the names of many prophets are known, but the teaching that is ascribed to them is actually that of seventh-century Islam.

4. Surprising Characters

Islam teaches that there were thousands of prophets. If you type the number 124,000 into Google, it is highly likely that one option that will suggest itself reads "124,000 prophets." If you follow it, you will find plenty of Islamic discussion about the number of prophets that there have been through history. That particular number is often quoted, but Islamic scholars answering online tend to be quite cagey as to whether or not it is reliable. Suffice to say, the prophets named in the Bible are not regarded as a complete list. The names that are attested in Islam include some which we do not expect. These surprises come under two headings. First, we have those who are mentioned in the Bible, but not as prophets—such as Adam, Seth, Lot, Isaac, Ishmael, Jacob, and Aaron. Then we have people from Arab folklore whom the Bible doesn't mention at all, such as Sho'aib, Luqman, Saleh, and Hud.

5. Prophets and Scripture

While it is understood that many prophets brought messages that were written down, it is generally taught that most of these documents were temporary or lost. Four prophets are said to have been given complete books, these being Moses, who received the *Tawrat* (the Torah); David, who received the *Zaboor* (usually identified with the Psalms); Jesus, who received the *Injeel* (the Gospel). Finally, Muhammad received the Qur'an, the revelation that replaced and ended all revelation. The scriptures are said to be "sent down"—that is, dictated word for word with no human component. The idea is that they are a duplicate of the divine original kept in heaven.

6. The Prophets and Perfection

Prophets are regarded as special, superior Muslims. They are held to be infallible, which follows from the idea that they are the mouthpieces for God. The sinlessness of the prophets is not an article of faith, but it comes as a shock to Muslims when we suggest that the prophets were fallible and sinful. If we glibly refer to a prophet as having been a sinner, our Muslim listener may be offended—for an attack on the character of a prophet is an attack on Islam, and an attack on Islam is an attack on all Muslims, including our listener. Nevertheless, it remains a fact that exploring the fallibility of the prophets is a vital avenue to understanding our need of God's mercy and forgiveness, so we need to know how to approach this subject. As it happens, the Qur'an provides plenty of evidence that the prophets did make mistakes and needed to be forgiven, although the average Muslim may not be aware of it.[2]

7. Muslims' Knowledge of the Prophets

Traditionally, Muslims have been quite content not to have too much information. Knowledge is for the experts, the religious professionals. Historically, enquiry into religious matters isn't generally encouraged, but today the internet is enabling more uncontrolled enquiry than ever before. On the whole, Islam is more about getting the practices right than learning history or even doctrine. Historic disputes within Islam have usually been about matters of law rather than truth. Muslims today come in all shapes and sizes, with every conceivable level of knowledge and interest in religious matters.

Why Do We Need to Know All of This?

We need to know this background information because some of it may come out in conversation. If we don't know where our Muslim friends are coming from, we risk misunderstanding what lies behind what they say. Likewise, if we don't understand what they are thinking, we won't know how *they* will interpret what *we* say. Our utterances can be 100 percent correct when they leave our lips, but if our words have a different meaning in their minds, then what they receive won't be the message we intended.

In our day, the stories of the prophets are becoming much better known—to the younger generation at least. Only in recent times has the idea of preparing story books specifically for children caught on in the Muslim world. With the rise of YouTube, it became possible to create short movies for children, and to make

2 For example, Adam, Q 7:23; Moses, Q 28:15–16; David, Q 38:24–25; Muhammad, Q 48:2.

them very accessible. Islamic cartoon versions of the prophets who have suitable life stories are now commonplace and can be found through simple online searches. Since the Qur'an always uses anecdotes about any particular prophet to support what it is being said about Muhammad and his message, such stories provide a way of presenting basic teaching in a child-friendly way.

With the exception of Joseph, the Qur'an itself does not supply complete stories. Back in the fourteenth century, when ordinary people were expressing curiosity about the prophets who came before Muhammad, an Islamic scholar named Ibn Kathir published what became a very popular book about the lives of the prophets. In compiling his book, he drew on the Qur'an, its commentaries, and other respectable Islamic sources, but some gaps he could only fill by going to the Bible. Modern storytellers, seeking to educate the new generation via animations, tend to draw on Ibn Kathir as the most convenient source. The English translation of his book is available on the internet.[3]

The widespread belief among Muslims is that the prophets were all models for believers to follow. It is taken as a given by most ordinary Muslims that all the prophets were without fault. But in reality, the Qur'an supplies plenty of evidence that this is not true. When I first arrived in Sudan as a short-term worker with a youth mission, Christians were exercising caution in what printed matter they were using. One particular group had been distributing booklets for some time that tackled head on the matters on which Christianity and Islam differed. The spark that caused the explosion was the circulation of a book titled "The Sins of the Prophets." It drew on Islamic sources, but it was deemed so controversial and subversive that the secular government of that time cracked down on them.

The Prophets in the Bible

When I ask Christians how many prophets there are in the Bible, many try to remember how many books there are in the section of the Old Testament called "the Prophets." We tend to think of the prophets as those who wrote certain books of the Bible—along with a few heroes, like Elijah. However, this definition is unnecessarily narrow. There are others whom we could quite reasonably refer to as prophets. Solomon wrote Scripture. Job heard God speak to him. Abraham never preached as far as we know, but on one occasion God specifically refers to him as a prophet (Gen 20:7). The blessings pronounced by Jacob in Genesis 49 were prophecies.

The characters that the Bible describes to us were far from flawless. The fact that they were fallible human beings who nevertheless were chosen and used by God is an encouragement to us because we too are fallible. Elijah, we are told in

3 For example, https://archive.org/details/StoriesOfTheProphetsByIbnKathir_20160627.

James 5:17, was a human being like us. The prophets received and transmitted the word of God, but they were never simple mouthpieces. Their distinctive accents come through. The word of God was lived out in the real world by real people. It was a partnership between God and man.

The testimony of the Bible focusses on God's saving initiatives, not on humanity's righteous response. God graciously speaks through the prophets, despite their failings. The prophets weren't superhuman examples who were impossible for us to follow. They were fallible human beings and recipients of God's grace and mercy. We can relate to them. All of this is very exciting for us, but it sounds rather suspect to Muslims for whom the prophets are supposed to be ideal role models, exemplars in word and deed.

I vividly remember a young Iranian woman talking about her religious studies at Oxford and reading Genesis for the first time. She was horrified at what she read about the behaviour of Abraham and of Jacob. She couldn't understand how such things could be true or how they could be recorded in a "holy book." For those with an appetite for reading at the academic level, I heartily recommend George Bristow's book *Sharing Abraham?*[4] He traces the fundamental differences between the concepts of prophethood found in the Qur'an and in the Bible, and then draws out the implications.

The New Testament encourages us to see the prophets as part of God's all-embracing plan. The gift of salvation was launched into the world on the foundation laid by the apostles and prophets (Luke 24:44; Acts 3:18; 10:43; Rom 1:2; Heb 1:1; Eph 2:20; etc.). The preaching in Acts often calls on the words and actions of past prophets. Even though Muslims are not taught the stories of the prophets as recorded in the Bible, and even though what they are told is often different from the account in the Bible, the names of familiar prophets provide a point of contact that we can use.

4 George Bristow, *Sharing Abraham? Narrative Worldview, Biblical and Qur'anic Interpretation, & Comparative Theology in Turkey* (Cambridge, MA: Doorlight Academic, 2017).

Chapter 4 Calling on the Prophets

Much of what Islam teaches about what God has revealed, about his prophets, and what he requires of humankind, we Christians are obliged to regard as untrue. The Bible and the Qur'an say different things about who the prophets were and what they did. Now, I know that I and many others with my background grew up with an instinctive desire to correct other people's errors, but that isn't the primary task God has given us. Our task is to share the good news of God's gift, new life for all in Christ. That will, at times, require some correction of faulty beliefs, but not the immediate and systematic correction of every error. Weary experience has taught me that arguing over secondary issues helps no one. It only damages the relationship which might have been a vehicle for grace. Once someone acknowledges Jesus as Lord, they are ready to relearn the rest. That doesn't mean that false beliefs are acceptable, but rather that there is a time and a place for tackling them.

The task we have been blessed with is to transmit the message of eternal life and proclaim Jesus Christ as Saviour and Lord. When we come across any group of people who have a significantly different mindset, it is helpful to use what common ground we can find. The goal is always that our Muslim friends will get to share in the grace of God made available to them in Christ.

Generating Opportunities

Theological discussions don't tend to happen by chance, and most people, both Christian and Muslim, wouldn't consider themselves adequately equipped to launch into one. Our desire is to bear witness, not to engage in theological discourse. How, then, does it help to consider the prophets? The first answer is that they can help us to create opportunities. For example, personal names come up in even the most mundane conversations. If you are talking to someone whose name turns out to be Musa (Moses), you can say, "Musa? What a fine name! You are named after a great prophet of God."

Such a statement does several things. Muslims tend to regard all Westerners as Christian and have learned from experience that most "Christians" are irreligious. This is puzzling and sad, but accepted as a fact. However, when we say something "religious"—the very thing we would avoid with our secular neighbours—we distinguish ourselves from the rest and show that we are people of faith. It shows that we might have something to say that is worthy of respect. It also shows that we are informed.

In addition, it gives our friend a chance to respond, which is very important. Muslims often feel that they are misunderstood and imposed upon. If we launch into premeditated preaching, it will do no good no matter how brilliant we are. We need to solicit their cooperation. We need to stimulate questions. Surprising them by referencing the prophets may do this. The way that individuals respond gives us a chance to assess what they are about. Are they spiritually minded? Are they hostile? How ready are they to talk about matters of faith? Are they wary of Christians?

My intent in this book is not to provide scripts to memorise and recite, but rather to provide ideas and suggestions for the reader to consider and adapt.

Some readers may be bemoaning the fact that it sounds like this is geared toward men. After all, the prophets were men. But the case is not as hopeless as it sounds. Muslim women usually have male names. Most Muslim societies use the patronymic system. A woman's first name is followed by her father's name, followed by his father's name. So Jameela Yusuf Ali is Jameela, the daughter of Yusuf, the granddaughter of Ali. And Yusuf is Joseph, which we may be able to use to make a link with the biblical Joseph.

Not only that, but mothers have sons and young women take care of little brothers, any of which may have a name that gives an opportunity. We just need a name to come up in conversation. Mothers love to talk about their children. And as we shall see, some common female names actually occur in Islamic stories about the prophets, although few Christians are acquainted with them.

Picking up on personal names is one way of generating an opportunity. Another would be to throw in an appropriate quotation or proverb with a prophet's name attached, or referring to an incident in a prophet's life. For example, there are plenty of moments in which it would be appropriate to say, "As the prophet Job said, 'The Lord gives and the Lord takes away. Blessed be the name of the Lord.'"[5] Or "'Man proposes, God disposes,' as the Prophet Solomon said."[6] Or when talking politics: "The government is ignoring the will of God, just as Pharaoh refused to listen to Moses." We can choose to bring the name of a prophet into conversation in a way that we simply wouldn't with a secular person. It is a habit we can cultivate.

Following Through

Knowing how to reference the prophets is not just about creating opportunities. The goal should always be relationship, not just a quick word. Expressing genuine interest in the person and putting the command "Love your neighbour as yourself" into practice may build the bridge that enables good news to be shared. An ongoing dialogue means more opportunities to speak. A knowledge of the prophets equips us with examples to use in reasoning. It provides us with stories through which we can communicate gospel truth. Being able to draw on such knowledge enhances our ability to communicate, but the most important factor in their assessment of our credibility will always be our character. We should never forget that even if we speak in the tongues of men and angels but have not love we are just making a noise (1 Cor 13:1). We cannot be reminded of that text too often.

Once in discussion, it is again useful to be able to draw on the prophets. The prophets, as individuals, have an authority for the Muslim which Bible texts do not. So, for example, if you say, "It says in Romans that all have sinned and fallen short of the glory of God," the statement has little authority, because they don't know what "Romans" refers to. It is the same for such terms as "Saint Paul" and "the New Testament." However, if you say, "The prophet Solomon famously declared that there is no person who does not sin,"[7] that taps into a recognised authority. The message is the same, but this time it comes with a reason to take it seriously. Being right is not enough. We need to be seen to be right. They do not need to be acquainted with the text to take it seriously. Most Muslims are painfully aware that they only know a fraction of the religious knowledge that is present in the world. The fact that the verbal statement has been attributed to a known prophet carries weight.

---

5 Job 1:21.
6 A paraphrase of Proverbs 16:9.
7 2 Chronicles 6:36.

Our intent should be to stimulate more questions, not to close down the conversation. If they ask where our words come from, we may have the opportunity to invite them to look at the Bible with us. We may have the chance to tell of or read Solomon's prayer in the temple, along with God's response (2 Chron 6:36–7:3). Solomon's prayer resonates with anyone who longs to have a secure relationship with God. God's response is impressive, but temporary. And of course, we know that the temple system failed to deliver. Today God has provided something better. If such a statement elicits the question of what we mean by "better," then you have the chance to speak of Christ, our high priest, and the Holy Spirit who fills us.

The prophets provide us not only with words from God but also living examples. Stories, if we know how to tell them, are much more interesting and memorable than mere statements. Presenting truth in story form is natural to most cultures. The Bible is full of stories for precisely that reason. We need to learn to use them.

Reasoning and Responding to Classic Objections

Muslims are taught well-known objections to gospel truth from an early age. They do not learn these things through reason, and so logical reasoning usually makes little impression. Since these objections are so universal, there is every reason to be prepared for them. Citing the prophets can help. It takes the conversation away from the tired, predictable arguments.

For example, how do you convince them that Christ died on the cross when they are sure that the Qur'an explicitly denies it? One reason that the denial of the crucifixion is so deeply rooted is because the idea of God saving Jesus sounds truer to them and makes more sense. Why would God allow a great prophet to be killed in this way? The story of Abraham's attempted sacrifice may help (see chapter 7). The sufferings of Joseph have already been mentioned in chapter 1.

Another example of a standard objection is that Jesus cannot be the Son of God. Simply pointing to a verse in which Jesus is called "Son of God' is unlikely to impress, but the promises of God to David in 1 Chronicles 17:7–14 give a different perspective on the question. If God was not speaking of Jesus, then who fulfils this promise?

Using the Bible

In many settings, the most effective way of using the Bible with Muslims is to be able to open it in their presence and to read it with them. Giving away Bibles or portions has its merits, but like the Ethiopian official of Acts 8 they often need someone to help them understand it. Quoting passages from memory may look impressive, but it does not compare with turning to a relevant passage and letting the book speak. To do that you need to know where to find potentially useful passages and how they can be used. Offering to show them what is written in the Bible opens up multiple possibilities.

The reason I began this section by saying that "in *many* settings" we can immediately read the Bible with our friends is because I have found that in some contexts, where Muslims are insecure or feeling under siege, they don't respond positively when we offer to show them something in the Bible. I found it easier to turn to the Bible in Africa than I do in the UK. In these situations, opening the Scriptures will have to wait until real trust is established and your friend is asking questions.

Before we get to that kind of detail, we need to consider some other general principles.

As a general rule, Muslims have been taught to revere holy books. That means that a holy book (in their case, the Qur'an) is only to be touched with clean hands, is to be put in places of honour, and is to be treated as a sacred object. Many Christians have different habits when it comes to how a holy book should be treated, and therein lies a problem. If we treat our Bibles in a way that *Muslims* think is inappropriate for a holy book, our actions will speak louder to them than our words. It will appear that we ourselves do not respect our holy book. The issue is not about determining who is right; it is about what we communicate both directly and indirectly. Carefully presented arguments defending the Bible's integrity are swiftly undermined by placing our own Bible on the floor or by having "added" to our Bible handwritten notes in the margin.

If you are asking God to use you in sharing the good news with Muslims, make sure you have a clean, unspoiled Bible or New Testament with you, preferably with the sort of cover that corresponds to its status as a "holy book" as opposed to, say, one with a cover designed to give it "street cred' with youth. You might want to consider wrapping it in a cloth too. If it is a pocket edition, keep it in a pocket above your waist. Never put it on the floor or place other objects on top of it.

There are well-rehearsed arguments about the validity of the Scriptures. For most Muslims, the most effective argument is to show the Bible to them and let them see or hear what it says. That requires us learning new habits in how we handle it.

Chapter 5 Adam

It was Friday, about the time of the midday prayers and weekly sermon in the mosque. Shareef was sitting in the park near his home in Northern England. I didn't know him well, but I did know that he had a troubled past and that he was seeking to leave bad habits behind him. Drugs had damaged his mind and he was on long-term medication. As part of his pursuit of a new life he had turned to Wahabi Islam and attended the most fundamentalist mosque in town. But on this particular Friday, he was sitting in the park with an open can of beer in his hand.

Here was a man with no delusions of self-righteousness. Shareef knew what it meant to fail, to be overcome, to be defeated. We talked about various things. Ramadan was approaching and he said he wouldn't even attempt to keep it. He said his medication exempted him.

"Think," I said, "of our great ancestor Adam. God created him perfect. He had no evil companions, no TV or movies to corrupt him. And with his own ears he heard the words of Almighty God. And yet with all that in his favour, the devil was able to lead him astray, to trick him, to defeat him. How much weaker are we, his offspring?"

Shareef looked at me. "Zillions," he said. "We are zillions of times weaker."

"All through history the sons of Adam have been defeated by the devil," I continued. "Even the prophets needed to keep asking for forgiveness. We all need God's mercy."

"Very true," Shareef said. "Even the prophets asked for forgiveness."

"And that is why," I said carefully, "God sent a second Adam."

I left that hanging for a moment. Whether he made the connection through what he knew from Islam or because he knew I was a teacher of the gospel, he replied, "Do you mean Sayyidna Isa al-Maseeh—peace be upon him?"

"Yes," I said. "Sayyidna Isa al-Maseeh—may his peace be upon us. Like Adam, he had no human father. He was different, and he was stronger. He was not defeated by the devil. He never needed to ask for forgiveness, because he never did wrong, as all the books testify. Satan fled before him."

"He did great miracles and healed all sorts of people," Shareef acknowledged.

"Yes, and he is alive and able to help people today too. We are all children of Adam through our birth, and so we inherit his weaknesses. But God sent a second Adam. We become joined to him by faith, and he shares his strength and his blessing with us."

Shareef looked away. He sighed and was quiet for a few moments. He gently changed the subject. But I knew he had heard and understood that I was saying Jesus was not someone who just brought more words. I had shown him that Jesus was God's answer to man's need and that he had power to make a difference. He had not disputed it. He had not yet come to the point of saying, "I want to know about Jesus; please teach me." But he was one step closer to that point. He did, in fact, come to church a few weeks later (his idea, not mine), an experience he still talks about.

Adam in Islam

First and foremost, Adam is regarded in Islam as a prophet worthy of great honour. He is a clear example of how the word *prophet* is more of a status than a job description.

According to Islam, Adam was created to be a *khalifa*—that is, God's deputy on earth. He was created on the sixth day of the week, which is reckoned to be Friday. Adam is said to have been fashioned from clay and then had spirit put into him. Eve is also known in Islam, and her name is *Hawwa*. Islam teaches that God created Adam first and Eve second. The Qur'an itself does not describe the creation of Eve, but her creation from Adam's rib is found within the Islamic tradition. There is no reference in Islam to Adam and Eve as being made in the image of God.

The Qur'an refers to what we call the Fall on several occasions (Q 2:30–37; 7:11–25; 17:61–64; 20:115–22). Some of the details correspond with the biblical account, others do not. Specific similarities include that there is reference to a garden, eating forbidden fruit, nakedness, and expulsion from paradise.

There are also ways in which the Islamic version differs from that of the Bible too. The garden seems to be a heavenly paradise rather than an earthly one, and the consequences of Adam's sin involved a descent to the earth. Satan plays a bigger and more explicit role than he does in Genesis. The forbidden tree is not identified in any way in the Qur'an itself. Different traditions identify it with various well-known trees (none of which is the apple!). The Tree of Life is mentioned (Q 20:120), but as part of the temptation.

The Islamic account of this episode of temptation is more about Satan than about Adam and Eve. God is said to have shown Adam as an object of wonder to the angels. God taught Adam the names of everything. God commanded the angels to prostrate themselves before Adam, and all of them obeyed except *Iblees*, the devil. Having said that, Iblees is said to be a *jinn* rather than an angel. His reason for refusing to bow down before Adam was that Adam was made from mere clay, whereas Iblees was made from fire (Q7:11–12).

God cursed the devil for his arrogance and disobedience (Q 15:34–35). The devil then set out to spoil things for Adam—to make him mortal and to get him expelled from the garden. He persuaded both Adam and Eve to eat from the forbidden tree. Adam swiftly acknowledged his transgression, and his repentance was accepted by God. Nevertheless, he had to leave the garden and live on earth. Satan is cursed, not the ground. The enmity between Satan and Adam's offspring is said to continue to the present day.

The Islamic version of the Fall provides an explanation for the human race living on earth and our experience of temptation by the devil, but it does not teach a fundamental break in relation between God and humanity. It also affirms the special status that humanity has before God as one created to worship him, serve him, and be his representatives on earth. At the same time, it affirms human fallibility. On account of that fallibility, people need guidance handed down by God through the prophets. Islam as a whole is understood to be the guidance given by God for human life on earth.

A link is made between Jesus and Adam (Q 3:59). Both are said to be special creations without a father. Adam also has a typological function—that is, to say the story of Adam represents the experience of any believer who may be subject to the whisperings of Satan.

Just because Muslims have heard of Adam, we should not assume that they know the biblical account, still less all the implications. They may not have much idea about the Islamic version either, but in the same way that most Westerners know that the Bible talks about Adam and Eve as the first humans, whether or not they read the Bible, so ordinary Muslims know who Adam is. They regard him as a victim of Satan rather than as the source of human sinfulness. That doesn't mean that our first priority is to correct them. Although this represents common ground to use, our objective is to point our Muslim friends to life in Christ.

For some reason, Adam is a popular name in some parts of the Muslim world, but not in others. It is relatively uncommon in the Arab Middle East and South Asia. *Hawwa* (Eve) seems to be a more widespread name.

Adam in Christianity

In Christianity, Adam is closely associated with sin and death. He is referred to in the New Testament in contrast to Christ (Romans 5:12–21 and 1 Corinthians 15:21–23 and 45–49). Strictly speaking, these passages are about the greatness of Christ, but they have also led us to take a dim view of Adam.

Before bringing the biblical Adam into our conversations with Muslims we may need to re-examine what the Scriptures actually say. The Bible accords the human race a high status—namely, being made in the image of God (Gen 1:26–28; 5:1–2). The Fall describes a loss of innocence and the forfeiting of life and privilege.

There are several interpretations of the Fall in the West. The medieval version, derived from Augustine, has all humanity stained by Adam's sin, in need of cleansing from it and inevitably sinful. We sin because we are born sinners; we do not become sinners because we sin.[8] This is the doctrine of original sin, a foundational truth in the West that was never fully adopted by the churches of the East. It is based on a reading of the Scriptures, but it is not the only one Christians have taken. Our modernised version has human *nature* corrupted by the Fall—meaning that the capacity to sin is inherited and perfection is unobtainable. We don't usually talk about being cleansed from what Adam did.

Another contemporary retelling of the Fall has Adam "dying spiritually," the result of which we are dead spiritually and need to obtain "spiritual life." Genesis 3 itself describes a change in awareness and hiding from God. Then God changes Adam and Eve's circumstances such that they no longer have access to the Tree of Life. This is the way in which the Hebrew expression "dying you shall surely die" (the literal rendering of Genesis 2:17) is fulfilled. The idea of being spiritually dead or spiritually alive isn't present in the text and we only find it there if we are looking for it.

---

8 A variety of views can be found among the early church fathers before Augustine in the West and later in the East.

In the modern West, building on the words of the Apostle Paul, many Christians have used their reading of the Fall as a necessary foundation to their understanding of salvation. In so doing, we have become accustomed to reading ideas into Genesis 3 which aren't there. One would be the idea of a total loss of relationship with God, whereas in Genesis God clothes Adam and Eve (3:21), sends Adam to work (3:23), Eve acknowledges God's help when she gives birth, and God speaks to Cain even after rejecting his offering. It is wise to be aware of this before opening the Bible with a Muslim friend and claiming the text says something that it does not explicitly say.

In the West, we have what is called a law-guilt culture. To grossly oversimplify the science of anthropology, human cultures fall into three broad categories. In addition to law-guilt cultures, there are shame-honour cultures and power-fear cultures. This has to do with how people process right and wrong. Genesis 3 actually addresses all three types of thinking. Adam and Eve disobeyed a law and became guilty. A consequence of having done wrong was an awareness of shame: they suddenly "knew they were naked." Hearing the voice of the Lord approaching, they experienced fear.

In the atonement, Jesus took the place of the guilty, the shamed, and the powerless on himself. He emerged at the resurrection beyond law, with the highest honour, and with the greatest power.[9]

The story of Adam and Eve also provides us with a moral example story. We see in the account how temptation may play out for any of us: doubting God, trusting appearances, listening to evil, and reaping the consequences.

The New Testament teaches that Christ is the second, or last, Adam (Rom 5:12–21; 1 Cor 15:21–23, 45–50). Just as sin entered the world through one man, so the new righteousness entered the world by one man. Just as death came through one man, so did life. There is a rich vein of teaching here. The passages themselves are quite heavy-going. They contain summary statements of ideas familiar to the first readers but not to us. We need to understand what is being taught here, and then weave it into our understanding of the rich fabric of salvation.

The majority of Muslims have been raised in a shame culture. Even those raised in the West tend to retain a strong shame-honour sensibility. This is not something that needs correcting. Most biblical characters display the same characteristics. Jesus confounded the legally minded Pharisees by shaming them rather than by arguing legal interpretation with them.

9 For a reading of Genesis 3 through the lenses of shame, see Simon Cozens, *Looking Shame in the Eye* (Downers Grove, IL: InterVarsity, 2019).

Calling on Adam in Our Witness

The following table compares the Islamic version with the biblical version, with differences in italics.

Adam in Islam	Adam in the Bible
First man	First man
Made from the ground (clay)	Made from ground (dust)
Honoured by God	*Made in image of God*
Eve made from him	Eve made from him
Lived in a garden	Lived in a garden
Deceived by the devil	Deceived by the devil
Banished from the garden	Banished from the garden
Became mortal	Became mortal
Repented	*Chastised*
Accepted by God	*Clothed by God*
Established the conditions under which we live.	Established the conditions under which we live.

The contrast between the Islamic and biblical views is not as absolute as some would make out. Some Christians argue that we must insist on convincing Muslims of original sin, forgetting perhaps that many of us came to Christ with a very incomplete understanding ourselves. As I noted above, the doctrine of original sin that Christians are often taught goes beyond what is explicitly stated in the Bible. I believe we have plenty to work with without requiring everyone to adopt a particular understanding of the human condition. We can work with what Muslims already know and believe.

We can honour Adam, as Muslims do, as the ancestor of our race, but then ask who has learned the lesson that Adam teaches us. God created Adam perfect. How great he must have been. Unlike us. He lived in a holy place with no corrupting company. He heard the voice of God with his own ears. Yet despite all this, Satan was able to defeat him. We, Adam's descendants, have fewer advantages and many more hinderances to righteous living. We are weaker. The devil defeats people today too. All around us we see evidence of Satan having power over people. We might invite our friend to agree with us at this point.

So God sent prophets to instruct people in the right way, but even the prophets asked God for forgiveness, because they too were descendants of Adam. That is why we need a second Adam. I thank God that he sent a second Adam. Who would that be?

It should be obvious. The man with no human father, the one from whom the devil fled (Matt 4:10–11), the one who never asked God for forgiveness because he never sinned. The one, in fact, who brought forgiveness *for* sinners. Jesus Christ.

This presents Christ as good news without having to argue about the nature of lostness. Every honest person knows they fall short.

We can go on to explain that by our natural birth we are all descendants of Adam. God sent Jesus so that we could have a new birth, a new life. God promises that if we put our faith in Christ, we receive new life and share in the blessings of Christ. Satan tricked Adam, and as a result Adam did wrong and became mortal and died. The second Adam, Jesus, is alive. We become people *in Christ* rather than people *in Adam* through faith.

As descendants of Adam, we need two things: forgiveness for our sins and power to live a new life. Jesus Christ brought both for all who will believe.

First Adam	Second Adam
Satan deceived him	Satan fled from him
Defeated by Satan	Defeated Satan
Dead	Alive
Brought death and judgment	Brought life and forgiveness

Because Adam is such a universal figure—the ancestor of all—he can be brought into many kinds of discussions. For example, in answer to the question, "Why don't you believe in Muhammad?" we can respond, "Muhammad claimed to be a prophet. Prophets are important, but what we humans really need is the second Adam. Prophets bring words, the second Adam brings change."

Such a response deliberately tries to invite the question, "Who is the second Adam?" If your Muslim friend asks that question, you can then talk about Christ rather than Muhammad.

Opening Up the Scriptures

Genesis chapter 3 is frequently called upon in explanations of the gospel. We get so used to interpreting it in the way that suits our presentation that we often lose sight of what it actually says. If we are going to read the passage with Muslims who have never read it before, it is hardly encouraging if we keep telling them it means something different than what it says.

- The passage mentions a serpent, and does not use the word *devil*.
- The passage makes no reference to freedom of choice.
- It makes no reference to different kinds of death.
- It makes no reference to spiritual realities as opposed to physical realities.

- No explicit link is made between bloodshed and the clothing made of animal skins.
- Two special trees are mentioned, not just one.

A lot of the ideas we read into the passage have to do with issues that arise for Westerners, such as why God would put the tree there if it was going to create a problem or why they did not die straightaway. These reasonings have a place in the Western context, and we are so used to these issues and our answers to them that we tend to confuse them with the raw material. Muslims will have different issues. We need to start again with the passage and let it tell its own message.

If the parallels and contrasts between Adam and Christ have been explained verbally, and our listener is interested, that is the moment to read Romans 5:12–21 and/or 1 Corinthians 15:21–23. I have found that 1 Corinthians 15:45–50 may be good for a more mystically minded Muslim who is looking to be intrigued rather than determined to nail down every detail.

Chapter 6 Noah (Nuh)

I saw a poster about a summer event which was being organised in a local church to raise money for a community charity. I went along to see who was there. I was surprised at the strong Asian presence in the front seats, as I knew the church to be overwhelmingly English-speaking white people. I soon became aware that there was no sign of anyone from the church at all.

The event was raising money for the *Noah's Ark Institute of Knowledge*, an after-school learning activity centre for children. Another name for it would be an independent madrasa—an Islamic school—where children learn the Qur'an. Usually a madrasa would run within a mosque, but this one was independent, operating in a small renovated industrial building.

Hearing this story, some Christians might suspect that some kind of deception was intended. Not at all. The story of Noah is included in mainstream Islamic teaching. Everyone involved knew perfectly well that this event was for a madrasa and would have been surprised at the idea that someone else might not have realised that.

Noah in Islam

Noah is known as *Nuh* in Islam, pronounced "Nooh," with an audible *h*. The story of Noah and the flood fits in well with the general thrust of the Qur'an. Noah is frequently depicted as a warning prophet,[10] not heeded by most of his audience, who then suffered the consequences. The focus is on warnings of judgement rather than on people being saved. In the Islamic version, Noah suffered ill treatment from the hands of those who refused his message.

In the Qur'an, those who board the Ark are a community of Muslims, including most, but not all, of Noah's family. One of Noah's sons doesn't believe and therefore drowns. He tried to save himself by climbing to higher ground. Popular retellings of the stories add other details, including Noah's passionate but unsuccessful intercession for his son. Many speak of Noah's wife drowning also. The Qur'an lists her as an unbeliever and a betrayer who was condemned to hell (Q 66:10), but it doesn't actually say that she died in the flood.

The reason for the flood is people's idolatry and failure to acknowledge God. The ark is called the *safeena*, which is the common Arabic word for a ship. Like Genesis, the Qur'an refers to people living for many centuries in the days of Noah. The gathering of the animals by pairs is recorded, and in the popular retelling many interesting details are added. I have come across stories about the first pigs being created on the ark to consume the droppings of other animals, which obviously strengthens the notion that pigs are inherently unclean.

Noah is remembered on *Ashura*, one of the Islamic holy days. It is said to be the day that Noah came out of the ark. It is also the day that Imam Hussain, grandson of Muhammad, was killed by his enemies. This is the primary event commemorated on *Ashura*, especially by Shi'ite Muslims.

Noah in Christianity

The story of Noah is found in chapters 6–9 of Genesis. The immediate cause of the flood is given as the evil behaviour and violence of humankind (Gen 6:5–6, 11). Some teachers also see the mysterious Nephilim of Genesis 6:1–4 as part of the reason. Perhaps because of the place of the animals, a simplified version of Noah and the flood has become a favourite for telling to children. Such renderings tend to end with the rainbow and not go on to Noah's drunkenness and the cursing of Ham.

The Genesis account has been used by preachers through the centuries to teach the certainty and finality of God's judgement, but that he also provides a way of escape for those who will hear and believe. The fact that God not only commanded the building of the ark but also sealed it himself (Gen 7:16) underlines that it is God who saves. People cannot save themselves. Today we too live in a world under judgement, and Jesus is the ark. In Christ is safety.

10 At least ten times: Q 7:59–64; 10:71–73; 11:25–49; 21:76–77; 23:23–30; 26:105–122; 29:14–15; 37:76–82; 54:9–17; 71:1–28.

Jesus himself referred to the story of Noah when he was talking about his second coming and about judgement (Matt 24:36–44; Luke 17:22–30). His emphasis was on life going on as normal until the sudden cataclysm falls upon the world. In 2 Peter 2:5, the story of Noah is used to underscore the certainty of judgement and the readiness of God to save the righteous minority. This is the only biblical passage that mentions Noah's role as a preacher. Most of 2 Peter 3 takes the flood account as a backdrop to the message that the world is just waiting for the final judgement, even though sceptics do not believe it. The judgement by water was but a token of the judgement by fire to come. The readiness of God to delay judgement so that people might repent and be saved is very much in view.

Calling on Noah in Our Witness

In Islam, all the prophets are in some sense "signs." It is therefore quite reasonable to ask someone how Noah is a sign for us today. We should, of course, be ready to give our own answer too.

If we keep track of Muslim holy days, we can use *Ashura* as an opportunity to compare our understandings of Noah and then go on to share how his story speaks to us today.

One area of common ground we may find with Muslim friends is the state the word is in—i.e., the many examples we see around us of people rejecting belief in God and his laws. We are living in a time in which the Muslim world is awash with talk about these being the last days. We can affirm that there is much in our day that is displeasing to God, and that the world is under judgement. We can also draw out "the testimony of Noah," which is that, though judgement must come, God also provides a way of salvation.

This allows us to ask our friends how they think they will do on the Last Day. What do they place their confidence in? We need not attempt to discredit anything they suggest; rather, we can ask if they are sure they will be OK. The answer is usually no, they cannot be sure, which gives us an opportunity to talk about the good news of Jesus. However, we should be aware that some traditions do hold out real confidence in Muhammad or in one of his representatives, so we shouldn't assume we already know what they believe.

For those who are in a state of uncertainty or are simply hoping their efforts will be enough, we come back to Noah, pointing out that he could not seal the ark himself. He needed something beyond what he could do for himself, and this came from God. The account of Noah demonstrates that God wants us to find the place of safety and to know we are safe. Those who were in the ark had no reason to fear. God has already prepared that place of safety for our time; and we enter it by faith in the living Lord Jesus, who did not come simply to preach like others, but to save.

The final judgement will come when Jesus returns and those who are "in him"—not depending on their own efforts—will be saved. Even Noah did not save himself; he believed the word of God, entered the boat, and God sealed it. The danger of being left outside of God's provision through refusal to believe is something we probably don't need to emphasise. The story they will have heard about Noah's son already does that.

Opening Up the Scriptures

In a conversation with Muslim friends about the state of the world, we might suggest that our days are becoming like those of Noah and then offer to show how the Bible described them. If our friends are willing, we can show them Genesis 6:5–6, 11–12 and ask them how close that description is to the world today. We might also ask if God was right to judge as he did. That might draw out a simple yes, in which case the way is open to talking about the present time and offer to show them what Jesus said about it (Luke 17:26–30).

If, perhaps as a result of secular influences, our friends have mixed feelings about the wrath of God, that becomes an opportunity to talk about God's mercy and patience. We might show them 2 Peter 3:3-10. This passage warns about scepticism, but it also speaks of God's desire for everyone to have the opportunity to repent and be saved.

Chapter 7 Abraham (Ibraheem)

Mahmood and I were sipping tea in my house in N'Djaména, Chad. It was a few days before the great *eid*, when Muslims all around the world commemorate Abraham's sacrifice of a sheep in place of his son.

"Tell me," I said, "Why is Abraham's sacrifice such a great cause of celebration for you?"

"Celebration?" he responded. "For some maybe, but I don't have the money to buy a sheep. No celebration for me and my kids."

"I am sorry to hear that," I said. "But I am asking what the eid is about. Why should people celebrate the event? What is so good about it?"

"Well, you know," he shrugged. "The prophet Abraham and Ishmael, his son. He was going to sacrifice him and then sacrificed a sheep instead."

"Yes," I said. "But what makes it such a major celebration?"

"We eat well," he replied. "People are happy because they get a good meal."

"I think it is very odd," I replied, "that Muslims everywhere celebrate it and make it such a big thing, yet they don't know the full meaning of what happened that day. We Christians have more reason to celebrate it than you do, and yet we don't."

"How do you mean?"

"When God brought Abraham to that place to offer his son, God provided the ram, didn't he? And then God caused it to be remembered this way all around the world. He did this because it was going to help people understand what he was planning to do for us later. He actually said to Abraham after he sacrificed the ram, 'Because you have done this, all nations on earth will be blessed through your offspring.' So it concerns everyone. What is the blessing God wanted to bring?"

Mahmood shrugged.

"The ram died in the place of the son of Abraham. Later, God sent Jesus Christ from the offspring of Abraham to become a sacrifice for the benefit of all people everywhere. He paid for our sins so that we might have the blessing God promised to Abraham. Now that is a reason to celebrate!"[11]

Abraham in Islam

Abraham is one of the most important prophets of Islam. He is mentioned seventy-two times in the Qur'an. He is featured in many Islamic stories; and in addition to being closely associated with Ishmael and the shrine in Mecca, Abraham is seen as the ancestor of the Arab people.

If you ask your Muslim friends what they know about Abraham, they will almost certainly tell you stories that you don't recognise from the Bible. Abraham is depicted as a man who rejected idols and stood up against the customs of his people. His own father was an idol worshipper, and Abraham firmly but politely proclaimed that only God should be worshipped. Abraham not only preached against idol worship; he destroyed the idols his people were worshipping. They wanted to burn Abraham alive, but God saved him from the fire (Q 37:83–99). Later, he and Ishmael would go to Mecca, rebuild the Ka'aba, and restore the true worship of God that had fallen into neglect.

Abraham is accorded the titles *Khaleel Allah* (the friend of God) and the *Haneef* (the monotheist), both based on Q 3:95. He is also called *Abu Deefaan* (the hospitable one), based on Q 51:24–27.

The story of Abraham almost offering his son as a sacrifice and God providing a ram in his place is well known and is commemorated in one of the major annual feast days, as I noted above. It occurs while the pilgrimage to Mecca is going on. The son is always identified as Ishmael, although the Qur'an does not explicitly name him in this role (Q 37:100–109). Abraham's experience is described as a test.

Overall, Abraham is seen as a great hero of the faith and a role model for the faithful.

---

11 See also the story told by Reema Goode in *Which None Can Shut* (Tyndale Momentum, 2010), 42.

Abraham in the Bible and Christianity

The name *Abraham* occurs 252 times in the Bible, 76 of which are in the New Testament. The biblical account of the life of Abraham runs through fourteen chapters of Genesis, from 11:10 to 25:10. Abraham is depicted as the biological and theological father of Israel.

The New Testament also looks back to the story of Abraham for the roots of the gospel (Gal 3:8). Jesus is described as "the son of Abraham" (Matt 1:1) and "the seed of Abraham" (Gal 3:16). The gospel is the fulfilment of God's promises to Abraham (Rom 4:1–25; Gal 3:15–18; 26–29). Abraham models salvation through faith (Rom 4:3; Gal 3:6; Jas 2:23). In Hebrews, the oath made to Abraham is fulfilled in the coming of Christ (6:13–20). He is held up as an example of faith (11:8–12). Abraham plays a significant role in salvation history.

Is Abraham a prophet in the Bible? Christians don't usually speak of Abraham in these terms, but the Lord himself did indeed refer to Abraham as a prophet in Genesis 20:7.

The Islamic narrative does not revolve around God making promises. The promises made to Abraham are not known. Nor is the idea of making covenants. Where covenants are mentioned in Islam, they concern humanity pledging to worship God, not God making promises to humanity.

Abraham in Islam	Abraham in the Bible
Born a pagan	Unspecified, but presumed pagan[12]
Turned from idols	Called by God
Rejected the idols of his father	Left his family and homeland
Father of Ishmael and Isaac	Father of Ishmael and Isaac
Ready to offer Ishmael as sacrifice	Ready to offer Isaac as sacrifice
Tested	Tested
Ishmael replaced by ram	Isaac replaced by ram
Called friend of God	Called friend of God
Called a believer	His faith was reckoned as righteousness
Rebuilt the Ka'aba	Was promised the land
A leader for humanity	Father of many nations
Hospitable	Hospitable

12 In the period between the OT and the NT, Jewish scholars speculated about the lives of the patriarchs and the prophets and wrote enhanced versions of their lives. In these documents, Abraham is much more heroic than he is in Genesis. Islam's stories echo these. The Apostle Paul distanced himself from this kind of material (Titus 1:13–14).

Abraham is honoured in both the Bible and in Islam. If we chose to speak of Abraham's failings, it is likely that Muslims will be surprised and even offended.

Calling on Abraham in Our Witness

When we acknowledge Abraham, it establishes common ground. Our expressions of appreciation for Abraham may help establish us as people worth talking to. If we can steer a path away from reinforcing or accepting a them-and-us position, the dialogue will be more fruitful. We should insist that we really do walk in the way of Abraham. He believed God, had a relationship with God, and did not follow some overly complicated religion.

Using Abraham to steer a conversation toward faith in Christ is relatively easy. For example, any discussion about Muslims and Christians gives us the chance to mention that we both look back to Abraham, and to go on from there. The whole idea of being, like Abraham, believers in an unbelieving world also gives us common ground. In addition, any context in which hospitality comes up gives us the opportunity of mentioning Abraham as a great example. And every year Abraham's sacrifice is celebrated at the eid, giving us an opportunity to speak of him.

The sacrifice story found in Genesis 22 provides multiple opportunities. True, the fact that Islam identifies the son as Ishmael is a stumbling block, but we don't have to trip on it. So many elements, even of the Muslim version, can be helpful to us. Specifically, it was God's command that there should be a sacrifice, that animal sacrifice was something God required, that God provided the ram, and that a substitute could take the place of the one destined to die.

At the most basic level, the story can be a departure point from common ground into neutral ground—unfamiliar truth that does not trigger defences. Islam says nothing about the role of sacrifice in the lives of the other prophets and its centrality in worship. This is a subject which prepares the listener to recognise that there are interesting things they don't know, and ultimately lays a foundation for talking about the cross.

The Genesis 22 story also provides a basis for answering the common objection that Christ did not die on the cross. The objection is only partly based on the words of the Qur'an. Its emotional power comes from the very idea that a holy prophet could be so treated. We can agree that the idea is shocking, but then explain how the plan and purpose of God was disclosed ahead of time through many signs, of which Abraham's sacrifice was one. We spell out how the son was helpless and couldn't save himself; it was God who provided the substitute. Once the ram had been slaughtered, Abraham's son knew he was safe and was deeply grateful. Another prophet of God, *Yahya* (John the Baptist), saw Jesus coming toward him and declared, "Look, the Lamb of God, who takes away the sin of the world!" (John 1:29). The fact that Jesus had the title "Lamb of God' is another piece of neutral information. This provides a way of reasoning that depends on storytelling rather than abstract logic.

If your own personal faith story revolves around the realisation that Christ died for you, then you have the possibility of explaining it by weaving in references to the Genesis sacrifice story.

Opening Up the Scriptures

Some of the Bible passages that refer to Abraham occur within complex discussions of theological arguments. This is true of Romans 4 and Galatians 3. I have found that taking someone straight into this kind of argument is unhelpful. It doesn't matter how true the text is if the person doesn't understand it. The presence of rhetorical questions in the text, and the assumption that certain things are already understood, make these passages quite difficult to use with someone who has no experience of the Bible.

In Matthew 1:1, Jesus is introduced, in the majority of translations, as the "son of Abraham," which provides an excellent jumping-off point. Other translations render it as "descendant of Abraham," which is excellent for secular English speakers but loses something for those quite at home with the idea that someone can be the "son of" without being the immediate offspring. I have often used this Scripture in response to questions about how we can describe Jesus as the Son of God. Instead of tackling the issue head on, I start with Matthew 1:1 and explain that Jesus has many titles and that all of them have meaning. I start with "son of Abraham"—the one promised by God to bring blessing to every nation. I intentionally delay getting to "Son of God" until the listener is ready.

In John 8:56–59 we find a passage involving Abraham which offers a way of talking about Jesus as much more than a prophet. This passage surprises rather than reassures, but it pushes past the idea that Christians mistakenly elevated Jesus to divinity. When surprise is expressed about his pre-existence, we can mention titles used even in the Qur'an, such as "Word of God" and "Spirit of God," which suggest something much more than a flesh-and-blood human.

For a serious enquirer, who is seeking to understand the message rather than simply to defend Islam, then it might be good to look at the links between the promises found in Genesis 12:1-–3 and 22:15–18 with the fulfilment found in Matthew 1:1, Acts 3:24–26, and Galatians 3:8–9. For good measure, you might go on to Hebrews 11:17–19, which brings in resurrection as well.

Ishmael and Isaac

Trying to prove that Islam is wrong about Ishmael is not a productive approach. It becomes an argument about whose religion is best rather than helping our Muslim friends discover what God has done for them in Christ. There is a place, however, for opening up the Scriptures with someone with whom we have a trusting relationship to see what the Bible says about Ishmael. What the Bible says is essentially positive. God promised to bless Ishmael (Gen 17:20). The contrast between Ishmael and Isaac is not between bad son and good son, but between blessed son and even more blessed son.

Start with Genesis 17:15–22. In telling the story, saying everything in the right order is less important than retaining the interest of our listeners by addressing what interests them. This passage shows clearly that Ishmael was blessed by God and loved by Abraham. Next go to Genesis 21:8–20, which tells of Abraham's regret at sending Ishmael away and God's intervention on Ishmael's behalf. If your friend wants to know more about the circumstances of Ishmael's birth, you can go back to Genesis 16.

Chapter 8 Isaac (Ishaq) and Jacob (Yaqoob)

Isaac and Jacob cannot be described as key characters in our witness to Muslims. They don't compare with Adam and Abraham. Nevertheless, they are counted as prophets by Muslims and may afford us some opportunities, so a few remarks are included here.

Isaac and Jacob in Islam

Isaac is called Ishaq in Islam, pronounced *Is-haq*, not *Ish-aq*. Isaac's name occurs eighteen times in the Qur'an, and Jacob's name is mentioned sixteen times. Isaac's name often appears with Abraham and Ishmael, Jacob's name with Abraham and Isaac's. Their stories are not told in the Qur'an.

The Islamic stories about the lives of Isaac and Jacob that I have come across draw heavily on the biblical account. The stories about Jacob skip over his lying and cheating. All prophets are required to be exemplary in word and deed.

Isaac and Jacob in Christianity

Little is said in Scripture about Isaac as an adult, and famous as his name is, he is generally given little attention. His place in salvation history is that he is the miraculous son of promise, rather than the son born by the will of the flesh.

By contrast, Jacob's story occupies a substantial section of the book of Genesis. His devious behaviour is told unapologetically, and his encounters with God are described in detail. God changes his name to Israel (Genesis 32:28), and his descendants bear that name. But even so, the name Jacob occurs many times throughout the Old Testament when the prophets are addressing the people of Israel.

Both Isaac and Jacob are dealt with in a single sentence in Hebrews 11:9, and they get scant mention in the rest of the New Testament. Paul refers to each of them in passing in his discussion about election in Romans 9.

Christians generally classify Isaac and Jacob as patriarchs, but not usually as prophets.

Can we speak honestly to our Muslim friends in terms of Isaac being a prophet? The closest he comes to prophesying is the pronunciation of blessings on Jacob and Esau (Gen 27:27–29, 39–40). Nevertheless, he was a man who received messages direct from God (Gen 26:24). He was recognised by others as a man of God (Gen 26:28–29).

Can we speak honestly to our Muslim friends in terms of Jacob being a prophet? He was clearly chosen by God, and he had remarkable encounters with God. In Genesis 49 Jacob blesses his sons, and in verse 10 he gives what is generally regarded as a prophecy about the coming of Christ. For these reasons, I would not hesitate to refer to Jacob as a prophet.

Calling on Isaac and Jacob in Our Witness

The name and person of Isaac offers some neutral ground. It speaks of something which is key to the gospel, but unknown and uncontested by Muslims—namely, that God makes and keeps promises. What is contentious, though, is Isaac's status in comparison to Ishmael's, as mentioned in the previous chapter. Nevertheless, as long as we are prepared to recognise the honour that the Bible ascribes to Ishmael, we may speak of God's promises, not only about Isaac but about the Seed of Abraham—namely, Christ.

In Genesis 12 God promised Abraham that through him all the families of the earth (i.e., all peoples) would be blessed. That was to come about "through his son." The son who was the bearer of the promise was born miraculously. Many prophets came from his line (uncontested information), and eventually Jesus too. He is the one who brings the blessing to all peoples. And those blessings consist of all that we enjoy through salvation in Christ.

Jacob gives us less to work with. As I said earlier, many things are true, but not everything is helpful in terms of bringing someone toward Christ.

One opening his name does give us is the story, recorded in John 4, that took place at Jacob's well. We could ask if they know the story of the woman who asked whether Jesus was greater than Jacob (John 4:12). Muslims should normally have no problem with the idea that Jesus was greater than Jacob, but it gives us the opportunity to retell the story of the Samaritan woman, along with the fact that Jesus described himself as the bringer of "living water" (John 4:10). It also gives an opportunity to discuss what kind of worship pleases God (John 4:23–24). In this case, the name of Jacob is simply the key that unlocks a door.

Opening Up the Scriptures

In Galatians 4:21–31 we find Isaac mentioned in relation to the gospel, but the contrast in Genesis is between two sons with different levels of blessing, whereas Paul uses Isaac and Ishmael (or more accurately Sarah and Hagar) as an allegory about spiritual freedom and spiritual bondage. The passage needs a lot of unpacking for someone who is not biblically literate, so I don't recommend it unless you have a very understanding relationship with the person.

Jacob's prophecy of Christ in Genesis 49:10 is not one that will be obvious to first-time readers of the Bible. They would be dependent on *your* explanation, not the words of a prophet.

Turning to John 4—the story at Jacob's well, mentioned above—with a Muslim friend has potential, but bear in mind that reading the passage will require some background information regarding the Samaritans. It gives an intriguing picture of Jesus interacting with the woman. He describes his purpose in ways unfamiliar to Muslim readers.

Luke 13:22–30 offers a good text to read with an interested person. It can be introduced by the question, "Who will get to eat at the table with Abraham, Isaac, and Jacob?" Jesus speaks of people from every part of the world being included, but the main thrust is a warning not to miss it. For the right person, this could be a great passage to look at together.

Chapter 9 Joseph (Yusuf)

Joseph in Islam

Joseph has the rare distinction of having his whole story recounted in the Qur'an all in one place. It is found in Sura (chapter) 12. The Qur'an is not primarily a book of narratives. Other important figures are mentioned here and there and parts of their stories are retold as fits the context of the passage; but for Joseph the whole story is told and has many similarities with what we find in Genesis.

In the Muslim world, Joseph is held up as a godly man who would not compromise the truth. His refusal to be seduced is very well known. He is seen as a role model for youth, especially for young men. The fact that he was finally vindicated and raised to a position of honour is taken to be a powerful message about Muhammad and Islam in general.

In recent years, several full-length movies have been made by Muslims telling the story of Joseph. As a result, even for people who don't read much, the basic storyline is well known.

Joseph in Christianity

Joseph gets more "column inches" in Genesis than Abraham, but he gets considerably less mention in the rest of the Bible. In the Old Testament, his name is used as shorthand for the tribes descended from his two sons, Manasseh and Ephraim. In the New Testament, Joseph is mentioned in passing by Stephen in Acts 7 and by the writer to the Hebrews in chapter 11. The remarkable parallels with Christ are not explicitly mentioned by New Testament writers, but one would imagine they were among the many things covered in Luke 24:27 and 44–45. Certainly they have been taught by Christians through the centuries.

Here is a list of the key similarities between Joseph and Jesus:

- A beloved son
- Publicly honoured by father (Joseph's coat/ Voice from heaven at baptism)
- Rejected by his brothers/by his people
- Sold by Judah/Judas (same name) for a sum of silver
- Handed over to Gentiles
- Regarded as dead by family/died and buried
- Unjustly accused and convicted
- Raised up to position of power and glory
- Able to save
- Was/will be revealed publicly to be alive
- Passed through sufferings so that others might be saved

Modern retellings tend to make Joseph guilty of pride in telling his brothers about his dreams and that his sufferings humbled him. It is true that in the biblical account Jacob, his father, was alarmed by the dream and the effect it was likely to have. But there is no criticism made of Joseph by any scriptural writer. The way the story is told in Genesis, Joseph behaved appropriately at every stage.

In Islam	In the Bible
Account starts with a dream	Account starts with birth (Gen 30:22)
One dream about family bowing to him	Two dreams about family bowing to him (Gen 37)
Jacob affirms and warns	Jacob rebukes and ponders
Brothers jealous, consider killing, conspire against him, and leave him in a well	Brothers jealous, react to opportunity, discuss killing, put him in dry pit
Joseph found by traders and sold	Joseph sold by brothers to traders
Brothers present Jacob with blood-stained clothing	Brothers present Jacob with blood-stained clothing
Jacob accepts serenely	Jacob is heartbroken
Joseph sold to an Egyptian (Aziz)	Joseph sold to Egyptian (Potiphar)
Master's wife (Zuleyka) attempts seduction and fails	Master's wife attempts seduction and fails

False accusation made and disproved, but Joseph chooses prison to avoid temptation	False accusation made and Joseph imprisoned
Joseph interpreted dreams about wine and bread in prison	Joseph interpreted dreams about wine and bread in prison
Forgotten and left in prison for years	Forgotten and left in prison for two years
Pharaoh's dream of seven fat cows; Joseph called and interprets	Pharaoh's dream of seven fat cows; Joseph called and interprets
Pharaoh investigates seduction allegation and clears Joseph	
Joseph volunteers to take charge	Joseph appointed by Pharaoh
The brothers come to Joseph. He demands to see the younger brother.	The brothers come to Joseph. He demands to see Benjamin, his younger brother.
Joseph places their gifts back in their baggage	Joseph places their money back in their baggage
Joseph greets his brother, accuses them of stealing goblet, detains one, discloses identity (some details differ from Genesis)	Joseph favours Benjamin, sets up test with goblet, eventually discloses his identity
Family reconciled	Family moves to Egypt and is reconciled
	Joseph recognises the plan of God to save his brothers (Gen 45:4–7; 50:20)

We are not in the habit of referring to Joseph as a prophet, but he received messages from God that he shared with others; so we need have no qualms about using such a title.

Calling on Joseph in Our Witness

Yusuf is a very common name among Muslims, and so provides opportunities to bring the biblical Joseph into our conversation.

The Qur'an says that Joseph is a sign to those who seek (Q 12:7). It is unwise to appear to present ourselves as those who know the Qur'an—because actually we don't. But we can certainly ask, "Is it true that the prophet Joseph is a sign to people?" And then invite them to tell the story as they know it.

Rather than focusing on the discrepancies, we can ask why Joseph was allowed to suffer in such a way. Surely God could have found an easier way to achieve the same results. Then we can explain how he is a sign for us. God allowed this to happen so that we would recognise what he later did in Jesus. He too was rejected by his people, betrayed, sold, and became dead to them. Then God raised him up to be their saviour, bringing them mercy. Joseph himself declared that he suffered so that others might be saved.

Since his story is so well known, Joseph can be mentioned in passing as an example of how a holy man can, in the plan of God, suffer to bring about the salvation of others.

Opening Up the Scriptures

The story of Joseph is told at great length in Genesis. It is possible to use it for a Bible study, but only with someone who is motivated to spend a good deal of time on it. On the other hand, Acts 7:9–10 gives us a very brief summary and is something we can open up on the spot, perhaps with the aim of moving from Joseph to something else. Psalm 105:15–22 gives another short summary, speaking of Joseph being sold as a slave and then raised up to instruct princes.

If we are telling the story of Joseph with a view to demonstrating that God allows his holy servant to suffer so that others can be saved, it's good to be able to support the claim by opening up a Bible and pointing to either Genesis 45:5 or 50:20 to underline that the prophet Joseph himself saw it this way.

Chapter 10 Moses (Musa)

I received a message from a local imam (mosque leader). "What do you think of Deuteronomy 18:18?" he asked. "Moses said that God will send a prophet *like Moses*. He told the children of Israel that this prophet would come from *among their brothers*. He did not say 'from among you,' but 'from among your brothers.' Muhammad—peace be upon him—came from the sons of Ishmael, the brother of Isaac. And Muhammad was like Moses in many ways. Don't you think that this verse is about Muhammad—peace be upon him?"

I thanked the imam for his question and arranged to meet him. This was not our first meeting, and I count him as a friend. The question was not new to me. It is often used by knowledgeable Muslims. I went to his home and found his Bible sitting ready on his coffee table, and we did some Bible study.

What is the most helpful answer to his question? Read on.

Moses in Islam

Moses is mentioned by name more than any other person in the Qur'an. He is best known for confronting Pharaoh, who in turn is seen as the archetype of a defiant unbeliever—refusing to submit to God and to his prophet. This example is called upon several times in the Qur'an as a parallel to the struggle Muhammad was having with the idol-worshipping leaders in his hometown. The reference is used to underline the inevitable defeat and humiliation of unbelievers. The Islamic version of the story has Pharaoh's wife believing Moses. She is named Asiya, which is a quite common Muslim girl's name.

Moses is also identified as the one who received the Torah (or as a Muslim might say, the *Tawrat*) from God. Muhammad is styled as the one who received, in a similar but better way, the more complete revelation—namely, the Qur'an.

Many other elements of the biblical story are found in the Qur'an, including Moses being raised in the royal household, killing the Egyptian, the incident becoming known, the flight to Midian, meeting his future wife at the well, God speaking from a fire, the signs given to Moses as proofs, his speech impediment, the appointment of Aaron, the return to Egypt (but meeting *the same* pharaoh there), Pharaoh's stubbornness, nine plagues (called signs), the departure from Egypt, the parting of the Red Sea, the tablets of stone, the miraculous provision in the desert, the golden calf, and Moses' request to look upon God.

These references are scattered through the Qur'an and not recounted as a single narrative. Each of these elements is given a distinctively Islamic interpretation. Completely missing from the Islamic narrative are the stories of the Passover and the bronze snake.

We shouldn't expect the average Muslim to be aware of these elements. For Muslims, Moses is primarily known as a model prophet, a warner of unbelievers, and the recipient of God's revealed law for the faithful.

In Islam, Moses is also associated with the mysterious figure of *Khidir*. A story is told in the Qur'an of "a servant of God' who instructs Moses (Q 18:65–82). Tradition gives this man the name Khidir. In the story, Khidir carries out a series of inexplicable and apparently malicious actions which baffle Moses. In the end, Khidir explains why these apparent acts of unkindness worked out for the good of the apparent victims. It is a simple story with the moral that God knows best and may allow tragedy to bring greater good. There are close similarities with popular Jewish tales, dating back to at least the third century AD, in which Elijah is the mysterious actor.[13] I only mention it here because as a Qur'anic tale easily taught to children, it is well known and therefore good to be aware of it in case it comes up.

Moses in Christianity

Moses is certainly a major figure for Christians. His story is taught to children, his example and experiences are explored by preachers and devotional writers, but theologically he is deployed in contrast to Christ. In Christian thought, Moses is closely identified with the Old Testament law as opposed to the gospel of grace.

13 See, for example, Barbara Diamond Goldin's *Journeys with Elijah: Eight Tales of the Prophet* (Orlando, FL: Gulliver Books, 1999).

Moses is always honoured in the New Testament, but the person and work of Christ puts him in the shade. The Apostle John remarks, "The law was given through Moses; grace and truth came through Jesus Christ" (John 1:17). In 2 Corinthians 3:7–18, Paul contrasts the covenant made through Moses with the new and better covenant made through Christ. "We are not like Moses," he declares in 2 Corinthians 3:13. The writer to the Hebrews makes explicit comparisons in chapter 3:1–6, declaring Christ to be immeasurably greater than Moses. Jesus himself makes a similar comparison in John 6:32–40. And at the Transfiguration, God the Father does the same, as the voice from heaven declares, "This is my Son. … Listen to him," as Moses fades away (Matt 17:5; Mark 9:7; Luke 9:35).

Jesus himself always speaks positively of Moses. He directs people to keep the law of Moses (referencing the *person* of Moses, not just the text of the Old Testament). Some examples can be seen in Matthew 8:4; 23:2; Mark 7:10; 10:3; Luke 16:29; John 7:19, 23. He also affirmed Moses, while correcting his listeners' understanding of what Moses meant—for example, in Matthew 19:7–8 and Mark 12:18–27. He may have contrasted himself with Moses, but he never positioned himself as being in conflict with Moses; rather he stated that those who truly followed Moses would also believe in him (John 5:46).

Calling on Moses in Our Witness

Rather than only presenting Moses from a Christian point of viewpoint, is there anything in the Islamic view which we can use? One way is to start with the agreed fact that Moses brought death to Pharaoh. Pharaoh heard the word of God repeatedly but did not turn from his own way. Then point out that we ordinary people actually have more in common with Pharaoh than we like to admit. Don't we know plenty of people who know the commands of God and maybe even teach them to others, yet fail to keep them? People hear the word of God and still don't obey him in every area of their lives.

Moses brought death to Pharaoh. We need someone who brings, as it were, life to Pharaoh—someone who transforms the disobedient into a true worshipper. That is who Jesus is. He calls to those who know they fail to please God. He brings them forgiveness, acceptance, and the power to live holy lives. That is Muslim-friendly exposition of the contrast between Moses and Jesus articulated in the New Testament, without in any way speaking negatively of Moses.

Law and Grace

Similarly, Moses is famous for bringing laws and commandments. That is great, but are laws enough for us? It was through Moses that God taught us that we should love God with all our heart, soul, and strength (Deut 6:5). Who can argue with the rightness of loving God utterly? But who can do it? And if we fail to keep this commandment, then we need something else. We need grace and mercy. The commandment shows us how great our need is. Jesus was sent to meet our deeper need.

The Bronze Snake

As I said in chapter 1, when we are talking about matters of faith, there are areas that are accepted by both sides, areas that are contested, and areas that are unknown and neutral. Raising something which Muslims are unfamiliar with about a person of interest creates possibilities for sharing about Christ. In John 3:14–15, Jesus refers to the story of the bronze snake. He spoke of it to someone who would recognise the reference and be able to apply it.

What we can do is to use the unknown story as a starting point, knowing that it leads us back to Christ. Rather than jumping in at the obscure (to Muslims) text in John, we can ask whether they have heard the story of Moses and the bronze snake. The biblical account is found in Numbers 21:4–9. Again, rather than reading it to them, we can retell it. People love a well-told story. A secular Western audience may well recoil from the idea of God sending poisonous snakes to afflict unhappy people, but a traditional Muslim—recognising that the people are giving verbal abuse to a prophet and expressing a scandalous level of ingratitude—is more likely to accept it. We need to set the scene in these terms. When the people recognised their wrongdoing and sought God, what did he do? He told Moses to set something up for them to look to.

They didn't need to be strong or clever or able-bodied. Nor did they have to do anything complicated or prove that they could be better people. There was no distinction between male and female or young and old. They only had to look upon the snake on the pole to receive their salvation. By looking, they were exercising faith in God's remedy for their need. They were putting their faith in God, not the snake. And do you know what? Jesus described himself as being like the bronze snake. He said that just as Moses lifted up the bronze snake in the desert, so will he be lifted up so that everyone who believes in him may have eternal life. And then we can ask them what they think Jesus meant.

A Prophet Like Moses

Many of those who have been trained to preach Islam to Christians like to quote the word of the Lord to Moses from Deuteronomy 18:18 more or less the King James Version puts it: "I will raise them up a Prophet from among their brethren, like unto thee, and will put my words in his mouth; and he shall speak unto them all that I shall command him." They take this to refer to Muhammad. They say Muhammad, like Moses, was the political leader of a whole community, who led them in war and in peace and was a law-giver. Moses engaged in a contest with unbelieving Pharaoh, as Muhammad did with the idolaters of Mecca. They go on to argue that "from your brothers" must mean from the Ishmaelites. If Moses had meant "from Israel," he would have said, "from among you."[14] This is despite the fact that verse 15 of the same passage does make it clear that the prophet will be from among the Israelites.

You may hear someone speaking in these terms, or perhaps even more likely, see it written in a tract or booklet given to you by a Muslim friend. How would you answer? Isn't it true that Muhammad was *more like* Moses than Jesus was?

The New Testament refers to this promise twice. In John 1:45, the fulfillment in Jesus is made explicit, but unfortunately the fact that Deuteronomy 18:15–18 is being referred to is not obvious to an uninformed reader. Acts 3:22, however, does refer to the text explicitly. We can tell our Muslim friends with confidence that we do not need to engage in an exercise of making comparisons between Moses and Muhammad, because the New Testament, the *Injeel*, tells us that Christ is the fulfillment of this prophecy. A point which we usually miss, but which I believe the apostles were well aware of, is that the Greek verb rendered "raised up" in Acts and that of the Hebrew in Deuteronomy can mean "raised from the dead," as well as "raised up/appointed." The message in Acts 3 turns on the fact of Jesus being *raised from the dead*. The backlash that follows in Acts 4 comes from the Sadducees, who did not believe in resurrection.[15] The apostles were described as proclaiming in Jesus the resurrection of the dead (Acts 4:2). This brings in a whole extra dimension to what the promise was saying about Christ.

These texts should satisfy any Christian unsettled by the Islamic claim that Deuteronomy 18:15 and 18:18 refer to Muhammad. The question remains as to whether these texts satisfy our Muslim friends. If they are inclined to be hostile, then they are likely to dismiss these verses along with anything else in Scripture that doesn't suit them. Inconsistent as it may seem, some will quote a biblical text as a proof for their argument, but then reject a different biblical text that we might use to answer their claim because they say "the Bible is unreliable."

In this kind of exchange, it is generally fruitless to pursue this line of response. Better to say that if they don't trust the Bible, then you won't have them quoting it at you; and then move on to a more useful track, such as personal testimony or just building the friendship to get past the barriers. There are answers to questions about text reliability, but they are not the focus of this book. Besides, it is pretty rare for a Muslim to come to Christ simply by rational argument. For a person who is seeking, resolving these issues may be a step along the way, but it is not primary.

14 Many more recent translations replace the expression with "from your fellow Israelites," which is no doubt how it was intended to be understood at the time.

15 Luke 20:27; Acts 4:2; 23:8.

Our aim is to point to Christ. One way of dealing with Deuteronomy 18:15, if it is brought up, is to agree that these words of Moses are really key, and to point out that they state that God commands us to listen to that prophet. Then we can point out the fact that "raised up" has two meanings, not just one. Jesus fulfils the prophecy on both levels, and that is the testimony of the *Injee*l (New Testament). We shouldn't quibble about Jesus being a prophet. As we shall see later, Jesus embraced that title. He is a "prophet-plus," not a "non-prophet." Jesus is the one Moses spoke of (and we choose to focus on the person, not the written word). We can offer to show them what Jesus himself said about it. The offer may be rejected by those who are closed anyway; then we will know where we stand with them. But if they accept our offer, we have taken a positive step together. We can then show them what Jesus himself said in John 5:46–47, which brings its own particular challenge.

Opening Up the Scriptures

Because of the many similarities between the Islamic and biblical accounts, there may be mileage in reading Exodus with Muslims who are genuine enquirers. They may not know the Qur'anic version very well, and will probably go hunting for it. Although there are differences in details, such as the number of plagues and which pharaoh was on the throne when Moses returned to Egypt, the most significant difference is the fact that God is so much more active in the biblical accounts. If we get the chance to read Exodus with a Muslim friend, then one of the questions that we should keep asking is what the text is telling us about God.

Reading Exodus together requires a season of reading. What about something manageable in a single session? You might turn instead to Acts 7:17–38, which offers a summary. Exactly where you choose to end your reading may vary as it goes on into less familiar territory. The passage has much that a Muslim should recognise, but the point that is being made in Acts 7 is that the Jews rejected Moses even though he was the one God had sent. The focus here is on *believers* rejecting him, not unbelieving Pharaoh. Acts 7:38 takes us to Moses' prophecy of the prophet to come, and from there we can turn back to Acts 3:22–26 to see who that prophet is. Just as the Jews initially rejected Moses, so they rejected Christ, whom God has sent. Acts 3:25 makes it clear that Jesus was sent for all nations, not just the Jews. These passages also make reference to Abraham and introduce the powerful theme of the promises of God, something Muslims are not taught and usually are not aware of.

Finally, for believers of Muslim background, the Passover story may be a very valuable framework for teaching. There is good reason to believe that it was used this way in the early church. In 1 Corinthians, Paul repeatedly made reference to aspects of the Exodus account, clearly expecting the believers to be familiar with the biblical story and to the Christian use of it. He refers to it as something they had been taught and should already understand. Read through 1 Corinthians and check for yourself. Paul's letter provides a narrative for describing salvation, baptism, and following Christ.

The this-worldly story of being slaves in Egypt, under an evil power, in slavery and unable to save themselves, illustrates the need for salvation and will resonate with what Muslims have probably been told about the children of Israel in Egypt. The story of the Passover lamb may be unfamiliar, but it contains echoes of the story of Abraham's ram. The blood on the wood of the door frame speaks powerfully of the cross. The meal in the house of safety is the basis for the Lord's supper, which is now filled with new meaning for us. The crossing of the Red Sea speaks of baptism. The pillar of cloud and fire alludes to the Holy Spirit. The journey into the wilderness speaks of life now.

Chapter 11 David (Dawud) and Solomon (Sulaiman)

She found herself in a room full of filing cabinets. As she explored her surroundings, she realised that all the files were about her, about what she had done, what she had said, what she had failed to do, and even what she had thought. Fear overwhelmed her. Uppermost in her mind was a desperation to destroy the records, but she found herself unable to do anything. The paper would not tear.

This is how a Muslim woman described a nightmare she had. She wrote about it in a Muslim family magazine. Whether it was a piece of fiction or a genuine dream, I have no way of knowing; but it was vivid and very well told. I remember sharing it with a number of Christian prayer groups without saying where it came from and asked them what they thought came next. Every time, my listeners expected some intervention from God or revelation of Christ announcing that he had dealt with it all on the cross. In fact, her story concluded with something like this: "I stepped out of the room and locked the door. I could never let anyone go in there." She then concluded the article with an exhortation to her readers to always do good and never do anything that they would be ashamed of.

I wrote a letter to the magazine. I expressed appreciation for the article, for it described the situation all people face, whether they take time to think about it or not. I then said that God was merciful and gracious. It was not his intention that we should live with such agony. I went on to quote from what the prophet David had written in the *Zaboor* (the Psalms): "Blessed is he whose transgressions are forgiven, and whose sins are covered. Blessed is the man whose sin the LORD does not count against him and in whose spirit is no deceit." I said that the prophet David received this blessing, and God in his mercy intends us to find it too.

The magazine published my letter. The quote is from Psalm 32, but I didn't write out the reference nor anything else distinctively Christian. I left it for thirsty readers to go looking for it.

David and Solomon in Islam

I am taking these two characters together partly because neither is as prominent in the Muslim world as some of the others, and partly because they are often mentioned in the same breath by Muslims.

Both David and Solomon are acknowledged as prophets in Islam. Muslims do not talk about David a great deal. He is mainly associated with two things. On is being the defeat of *Jaaloot*, which we take to be Goliath. A king named *Taaloot* is also mentioned, who is presumably Saul, the king of Israel at the time. Elements of the story in the Qur'an seem to have been picked up from the story of Gideon (see Q 2:246–51). The second thing that David is known for is that he "received" the *Zaboor*, a holy book, usually understood to be the Psalms (Q 4:163; 17:55).

The fact that David was a king is stated in the Qur'an (Q 2:251, 38:17–20), but it isn't necessarily something that the average Muslim is aware of. The Qur'an has a very oblique reference to David's sin with Bathsheba (Q 38:24–25), but most Muslims don't know the story and are horrified at the very suggestion. All prophets, they are told, lived exemplary lives.

Although Solomon is only mentioned a few times in the Qur'an, he occupies a much bigger place in Muslim folklore. He is known as "Solomon the Wise" (*Sulaiman al-Hakeem*), and is said to have been able to converse with birds (Q 27:16). He is also said to have had a vast army under his command, comprised of men, spirit beings (*jinn*), animals, and birds. This is referred to briefly in the Qur'an (Q 27:17–19), but stories about Solomon are developed extensively elsewhere. He is in Muslim culture an almost fairy-tale character.

Perhaps the story about Solomon that is most widely known is his meeting with the Queen of Sheba, which is found in the Qur'an (Q 27:20–44). The text has significant embellishments not found in the Bible, and the story has yet more added to it in popular folklore. All Muslims know that the queen's name was

Bilqis (or Balaqeesa, in some languages), although her name is not supplied in the Qur'an.

In the Islamic account, Solomon learns of the queen and her magnificent throne from a bird with whom he talks. He hears that Bilqis and her people have been led astray by Satan to worship the sun. He sends the bird back with a letter calling her to submit to the true religion. While the queen is on her way to visit him, Solomon sends a mighty jinn to get her throne and place it in his palace. She becomes a Muslim and one of Solomon's wives.

David and Solomon in Christianity

David and Solomon are both major Old Testament figures. David's trials and tribulations are given in considerable detail, providing plenty of material for preacher and devotional writer alike. He is, of course, famous for his military victories and for writing many of the Psalms. The story of David and Goliath is iconic and is known far beyond Christian circles. His adultery with Bathsheba and his subsequent repentance is also a very powerful story for Christians.

Less is said in the Bible about Solomon, nor does he feature so strongly in Christian teaching. He is best known for the gift of wisdom which he received and the temple which he built. The fact that, despite his great wisdom, he was led astray by his wives greatly diminishes his status as a hero of faith.

David's name appears much more frequently in the New Testament than Solomon's. In fact, David's name appears in both the first and last chapter of the New Testament. This is because the very concept embodied by the word *Messiah*, or *Christ*, is strongly tied to David. It is no accident that Jesus is greeted as "Son of David' by those who believe in him. It was to David that the promise was given that one would come from his offspring who would be God's Son and set over God's everlasting kingdom (1 Chr 17:1–15). The apostles found references to Christ in David's psalms (e.g., Acts 2:25 and 4:25). The very notion of the Messiah was rooted in the words of David. Jesus himself quotes David when he discusses the identity of the Christ (Matt 21:41–46).

In the New Testament, Solomon is mentioned almost in passing. The flowers of the field are more glorious than Solomon's splendour in Matthew 6:29 and Luke 12:27. Jesus contrasts the indifference of the people of his time with the readiness of the Queen of Sheba to travel a long distance to hear Solomon (Matt 12:42; Luke 11:31), adding that he himself was greater than Solomon. Solomon is never mentioned in the letters of the New Testament, which again is in contrast to David.

Christians do not habitually refer to David or Solomon as prophets, but rather as kings. Nevertheless, David is explicitly identified as a prophet in Acts 2:30, and implicitly by Jesus in Matthew 22:43. Solomon is never accorded that title. However, he contributed to the writing of the Scriptures: Proverbs, Ecclesiastes, and Song of Songs. That is enough for me to refer to him as a prophet when I am talking with Muslims.

Calling on David and Solomon in Our Witness

As I mentioned earlier in the chapter on Abraham, whenever a Muslim raises the question of Jesus being the Son of God, I nearly always go to the first verse of the New Testament. As well as referring to Jesus as "the son of Abraham," Matthew 1:1 calls Jesus "the son of David." I often say that Jesus has many titles, and until you understand what "the son of David" means, you won't understand the others. That might sound like I'm dodging the question, but I'm not. It allows me to apply a filter. If the person really wants to know, they will let me continue. If they reject the beginning of my answer, I know that they aren't open to listening and I need to change the subject.

If we are able to continue with the son of David theme, I am able to navigate some neutral ground, something that they have not been taught to reject out of hand. I can explain how God promised David that he would send someone who would be a great king and saviour and who would rule forever. This great king is the true king of all believers. Jesus didn't simply come to tell people that God is one. He came to initiate God's kingdom promised by the prophets. In fact, God said something very mysterious to David. Concerning that descendant of David, he said "I will be his father and he will be my son." Who could he be referring to if not Jesus? Such an approach opens up multiple lines of enquiry and is very much teaching about the person and work of Jesus.

The central theme of this book is appealing to what the prophets themselves said or did. David's psalms give us plenty to work with. I mentioned Psalm 32:1–2 earlier in this chapter. We can drop David's name into a conversation about worship and prayer. David gives us great prayers. "Create in me a pure heart, O God, and renew a steadfast spirit within me" (Ps 51:10). That expresses a sentiment that many devout Muslims respond to. There are many other verses in the Psalms that do the same thing. "Know that the LORD is God. It is he who made us, and we are his" (Ps 100:3). "Praise the LORD, O my soul; all my inward being praise his holy name" (Ps 103:1). Whether we remember the references is secondary. The important thing is to quote David and identify him as the source.

Referring to these verses and others like them both marks us as people who are serious about God and creates a platform for deeper conversation. Hopefully this will give a glimpse of a deeper level of relationship with God than they have found to be available to them. These words speak to the needs of the heart. The fact that these lines come from a known prophet gives them added credibility. It may lead to our friend asking to see or to have a Bible.

David can also be called on when we are talking about the state of the world. "The fool says in his heart, 'There is no God'" (Ps 14:1). This is by no means the only example of David bemoaning the presence and power of those who don't fear God.

Solomon also gives us something to work with. As I mentioned in chapter 3, he declared that there is no person who does not sin (1 Kgs 8:46). Solomon is a much more relevant person to refer to when talking to Muslims than the Apostle Paul.

I have obtained artistic presentations of Proverbs 3:5–6, framed them, and used them as gifts for Muslim friends. I present them as the words of the prophet Solomon the Wise. I know an imam who has that text in pride of place in his sitting room. It is a reassuring promise, but also a challenge to go on seeking, especially since it comes from the Bible rather than an Islamic source. I wonder how many guests the imam has had to tell that the text comes from the Bible.

Of course, the most tellable story about David is the killing of Goliath. Islamic stories refer to it, but don't usually tell the story in a way that presents its full drama. As Christians, we should be ready to tell that story in a way that lays a foundation for sharing how Christ has defeated evil. He tackled the apparently invincible foe by coming in weakness. We all need such a Saviour and God has sent one for us all.

Opening Up the Scriptures

There are many possible settings in which we could ask a Muslim friend, "Would you like to see what the prophet David wrote?" We can then turn, for example, to Psalm 23, which describes David's relationship with God. The psalm is not a set of instructions; it is a testimony. Reading Psalm 23 together can then be a basis for sharing something of our own experience. We might go from there to sharing how Jesus came to be the Good Shepherd for all, how his sheep hear his voice, and how he laid down his life for those who follow him (John 10:1–21).

If you have a favourite psalm, think about how you might introduce it and read it with a Muslim friend, and then how you would share what it means to you. Don't worry if they initially reinterpret it in their own Islamic context. Let them "taste and see," and pray that the Lord draws them back to the Scriptures. Psalms 4, 8, 27, 32, 42, 100, and 139 would all be very suitable. However, beware of psalms that focus on Zion or Israel, for the simple reason that such psalms are liable to be misunderstood and/or lead to a political conversation. There is a place for such conversations, of course, but they don't tend to bring people to Christ.

Another text to turn to with a serious enquirer is Acts 2:25–36. This passage both quotes David and places him in contrast to the much greater person of Jesus, risen from the dead.

Chapter 12 Jonah (Yunus) and Job (Ayyub)

I boarded the bus at about 4 a.m. It was about an hour and half before dawn. We were about to set off on a journey of well over 500 miles across Chad. As I made my way to my allotted seat, I saw a man playing chess on a tablet. I will call him Usman. I greeted him in Arabic, and to my surprise he answered in English. My seat was in the row immediately in front of him, so I turned and chatted with him in the few minutes before we set off.

I learned that Usman had spent more than fifteen years living in the West, but his circumstances had changed and he had been obliged to return to his country of birth. His home was now in the obscure town, on the edge of the Sahara, where he had been born. He had left his religion behind long ago, but in this new phase of life he was embracing it and making up for lost time. By the way, chess is one of those activities banned under one school of Islamic law but accepted under another. He may not have known that.

The final passengers took their places and the bus moved off. After about an hour, clear of the city, the bus pulled over so that the passengers could get off to pray the mandatory pre-dawn prayer. I looked around and saw that my new friend was staying put and looking uncomfortable.

"Are you not going to pray?" I asked.

"I can't," he replied. "I performed my ablutions [required before praying] before I got on the bus. A woman has been sitting close to me, touching me in fact. So I need to perform the ablutions again and I don't have any more water with me."

Indeed, a woman had been seated next to him, veiled up to the eyes. There had been no skin to skin contact, but it seemed that even his clothes touching her clothes was a problem for him.

"Aren't you permitted to use clean sand when water is not available?" I asked.

"Yes," he answered, "but look outside. There is cattle dung everywhere. The sand is not clean."

"Listen to me," I said. "God would not reject your prayer simply because you have no water."

"But Islam teaches . . . " he began, but I interrupted him. He was, after all, used to Western manners. "I know what Islam teaches. I am telling you that I know God. I know what he is like. He would not reject anyone for simply not having water. He looks at the heart."

"But Islam teaches that I must be ritually clean to pray," he responded.

"The prophet Jonah prayed in the belly of the whale," I countered. "God heard his prayer and delivered him. Think about it. But if you really think you need water, you are welcome to take mine." I handed him my drinking water.

"Thank you," he said, and then got off the bus.

Some weeks later, I heard from a Christian worker who lived in Usman's hometown. Usman was regularly attending a Bible study.

I am taking these two characters, Jonah and Job, together for convenience, not because there is any particular link between them. They each deserved to be mentioned, but they don't merit a whole chapter each.

Jonah in Islam

Jonah (*Yunus*, or sometimes *Yunis*) is a common name in the Muslim world. The Islamic version of his story tells of his being swallowed by a whale (Q 37:139–48; 68:48–50). He is understood to have been sent to the people of *Ninowa* (Nineveh). This retelling conforms to the Islamic understanding that each prophet is sent to a people. In the Islamic version, Jonah is swallowed by the whale *after* preaching in Nineveh. The people had refused to repent, so Jonah became angry and left them. Then comes the journey, the storm, and the whale. God causes a plant to shade Jonah while he was recovering from his ordeal. Finally, the people do repent and accept him as a prophet. Most of the elements of the biblical account are present, but the order of the events and the thrust of the story are different.

Muslims, in common with us, see Jonah's story as one that children can easily relate to, so it appears in Islamic children's books and increasingly in cartoon form on YouTube. Since most forms of Islam forbid creating images of the prophets, don't be surprised if Jonah's face is blurred.

While in general Muslims emphasise the perfection of the prophets, Jonah is recorded as acknowledging his faults, admitting that he was a "wrong-doer" (Q 21:87). I am indebted to my friend Jan Pike for informing me of a discovery she made. She found out that some Muslim women make it a regular practice to end each day by praying the "prayer of Jonah," drawn from that passage in the Qur'an. This came to light through using the programme she developed, which gets Muslim women and Christian women to talk about the prophets together.[16] What is particularly interesting, is that in the experience of both Jan and myself, many Muslims are happy to talk about God being ready to forgive, but we rarely hear them identify themselves as sinners.

Jonah in Christianity

The story of Jonah and the whale is well known even outside of Christian circles. Parts of it are frequently used as a children's story, but not so many people are aware of Jonah's prayer in the second chapter. Jonah's behaviour in the fourth chapter is also less well known, but it gives real pause for thought. The biblical story ends in a somewhat open and unsatisfactory way for the modern reader. Perhaps it is intended to leave uncomfortable questions hanging in the air.

Debates about whether Jonah was rescued by a whale or a large fish, whether it is possible for someone to survive inside a whale/fish, and whether the account is to be taken as history or fable are frequent and largely beside the point. The story is about God, who is actually the principal actor, his human servant, and lost people. God wants the people to repent. Jonah, like so many believers, had mixed feelings about involving himself in God's mission. I have lost count of the number of times I have heard testimonies in which someone has realised they were like Jonah, fleeing the call of God.

Jonah is referred to by Jesus in two contexts. One is to contrast the readiness of the people of Nineveh to respond to Jonah, as against the poor response of his own people, even though he himself was greater than Jonah (Matt 12:41; Luke 11:30–32). The other context concerns Jesus' own burial and resurrection, of which Jonah's experience was a sign (Matt 12:39–4). Other than these two instances, Jonah is not mentioned in the New Testament.

Calling on Jonah in Our Witness

The Qur'an weaves the story of Jonah into something that commends Muhammad and promotes Islam. Our challenge is to use it to point to Christ and to a biblical understanding of who God is and what he is like. As far as possible, we want to do that from what our friends know rather than arguing about details and sequences.

16 See http://prophetstories.org.uk/.

The story of Jonah shows that God gives people second chances, a subject that may easily arise in conversation with a friend. It can also be used, as above, to suggest that ritual washing is not really what God cares about.

It would not be unreasonable to ask a friend who is a faithful Muslims if he or she knows or uses the prayer of Jonah. If they do, we might comment that if a prophet needed to pray like that, how much more do we? We might then tell them the story Jesus told about the Pharisee and the tax collector (Luke 18:9–14), and the fact that Jesus came that sinners might find forgiveness. The religious man in the story might have assumed he was accepted by God because he was so devout, but identifying ourselves as sinners before God is encouraged by Jesus.

In a conversation with someone we have been sharing with for some time (rather than as a conversation starter), we can ask them if they know that Jesus referred to the sign of Jonah and what it means. Referring to a prophet as a sign is common currency in Islam. If they say no, we can explain that Jesus said that as Jonah was three days in the belly of the whale/huge fish, so he himself would be buried for three days and then rise again.

However, if your friend has undergone training in apologetics, he or she might say they do indeed know about the sign of Jonah. There are booklets in circulation written by a very confrontational Islamic preacher named Ahmad Deedat. He was a member of the *Ahmadiyya*, a sect utterly rejected by most Muslims. His treatment of the sign of Jonah reflects his sect's minority view that Jesus didn't die on the cross but was buried alive and able to make his escape. Despite not reflecting orthodox Muslim teaching, his booklets are widely circulated among orthodox Muslims. You can find a full Christian rebuttal of Deedat's booklet by googling "John Gilchrist. What was the sign of Jonah?"

Opening Up the Scriptures

The book of Jonah brief. It can quite easily be read through with an interested person in a single sitting, or divided into two or four sessions. The important thing is to let the text speak for itself by asking open questions, such as "What does the passage tell us about God," "What does it say about his servants?" and "What is it saying about humanity as a whole"—all with the aim of having God show us how we need to change.

Job in Islam

Job (*Ayyub*, pronounced *Ayyoob*) is known in Islam as the prophet who was severely tested and remained faithful. The Islamic version contains many of the elements found in chapters 1 and 2 of the biblical account, but somewhat embellished. Job's wife (Raheema) plays a bigger and more positive role than in the Bible, though at one point Job does give her a beating! The idea that God allows suffering as a test is very current in Islam, and Job is used to illustrate that understanding.

Job in Christianity

The patience of Job is of course proverbial. His story is used as an example of patience in affliction and trusting God when such affliction seems to make no sense. Job is only mentioned once in the New Testament, in James 5:10–11, where he is referred to as showing great patience and ultimately being rewarded for it.

Calling on Job in Our Witness

A question we can ask to introduce a helpful direction with reference to Job is to ask if our Muslim friend knows of Job's famous testimony. The answer will probably be negative. Our answer is that Job declared that he knew that his redeemer lived and would stand upon the earth (Job 19:25). He called God "his redeemer," an unfamiliar term for Muslim people that invites explanation and that leads to the question of how his redeemer, the one who sets him free, in this case God, could stand upon the earth. The answer, of course, is that God came in the person of Christ to redeem people of every tribe, nation, and tongue.

Job, like Joseph, was a prophet who suffered. If we ask who benefited from his suffering, we are likely to be told that he suffered as an example for us all. That enables us to point out that in certain circumstances God does indeed allow his holy prophets to suffer for the benefit of others, and that is exactly what Jesus said would happen to him. If such an opening provokes a question, you have a basis for talking about how Jesus chose the cross out of love for us, but never forget to include the vindication too—the resurrection.

Opening Up the Scriptures

The book of Job has the unusual distinction of containing long sections that are not true, or to put it more accurately, the speeches of his friends which contained a certain amount of wisdom, but which in the end God himself rejected (Job 42:7–9). This makes it a difficult book to use for a Bible study with a Muslim friend.

James 5:10–11 gives a very brief summary of Job's story, placing the accent on the positive. If you meet someone with *Ayyub* as part of their name and want to use that as an opportunity to show them the name in the Bible, this would be a good passage to turn to.

Chapter 13 John the Baptist (Yahya) and Zechariah (Zakariya)

The preacher quoted the words of John the Baptist as found in John 1:29: "The next day John saw Jesus coming toward him and said, 'Look, the Lamb of God, who takes away the sin of the world!'" Then he eyed the congregation and asked them how many Muslims were mentioned in that text. Being a fairly typical English congregation, they looked puzzled but polite. This had to be a trick question. Obviously, there were none at all. Pushed for an answer, someone responded with a questioning tone: "None?"

"Correct. That is the correct *Christian* answer," said the preacher, further puzzling the congregation. "But according to Islam, both John the Baptist and Jesus were Muslims; so according to that way of thinking, there were two."

The congregation relaxed. The eccentric preacher had enjoyed his little joke. He continued, however: "But God's answer is different again. How many Muslims are mentioned in the passage? God's answer is *all of them*. The Lamb of God who takes away *the sin of the world*—everyone—every tribe, nation, and tongue. The Lamb of God was sent for all the Muslims."

John the Baptist and Zechariah in Islam

John the Baptist is referred to in Islam as Yahya son of Zakariya. Nothing is said of him baptising anyone. He plays a very minor role in Islamic teaching. The Qur'an gives an account of his birth (Q 3:39–41; 19:1–15), which echoes some elements of Luke 1:5–22 and 1:57–66, such as the age of his parents, barrenness of his mother, that his name was not a family name, Zechariah losing the ability to speak, though without any hint of failing to believe.

The Islamic world has some stories about John that are not in the Qur'an, but they are not particularly widely known. It is possible that they may become better known as a result of the rise of online, animated prophet stories for children, as I mentioned previously. The traditional stories that do exist depict John as a mystic: eating little, shunning company, living in voluntary poverty, and devoted to God at a very young age. He is said to have befriended wild animals. Islamic teaching speaks of John's death at the hands of a wicked king as a favour to a woman, and that God punished them in response.

Zechariah is acknowledged as a prophet in Islam. He is identified as John's father, but his main role is as the guardian of Mary, the mother of Jesus, which is related in the Qur'an (3:37).

John the Baptist and Zechariah in Christianity

John is mentioned in all four Gospels and in Acts, and is seen first and foremost as the forerunner of Christ. Jesus speaks highly of him (Luke 7:24–35), but also says that the least in the kingdom of God is greater than John (Luke 7:28). Accordingly, Christians tend to speak of John only with reference to Jesus. He is explicitly identified as a prophet in Luke 1:76 and 7:26.

Zechariah is mainly known for his part in the story of John's birth, which is often read in the Advent season. In Luke 1:67–79, Zechariah is filled with the Holy Spirit and prophesies, so it is quite appropriate to refer to him as a prophet.

Calling on John in Our Witness

Because John's name is honoured but yet little-known, we have some neutral ground to work with. However, we need to be aware that the name Yahya bears so little resemblance to John that we will need to explain that we are talking about the same person—the son of Zechariah. Referring to him as "the Baptist" will not help Muslims identify who we are talking about.

Simply starting with the mention of John's name (Yahya), we can describe his ministry in the desert and the call to repentance that he issued. We can describe and explain his use of baptism. While the act of baptism is usually unfamiliar to our Muslim friends, the notion of calling people to turn away from their sins will strike a chord as entirely appropriate for a prophet; and in that context, baptism as a washing away of the past and starting a new life makes sense. We can tell that story with a variety of end points in mind.

One potential end point is to talk about John's proclamation that the one who is coming after him is greater because John only baptised with water for repentance and the coming one would baptise with the Holy Spirit. This gives us the opportunity to affirm the importance of repentance in general, but also to explain that repentance is only a preparation for receiving something greater from God, the gift of the Holy Spirit. This takes us from the familiar—the necessity of repentance—to the unfamiliar and therefore uncontested—the gift of the Spirit. A listener with a responsive heart should feel the need to ask more about the Spirit. This gives us the opportunity to open up that particular aspect of salvation, the gift of the Spirit, that comes through Christ.

Another direction we can take with the story of John baptising Jesus revolves around the voice of God (Matt 3:17). We tell the story, including John's reluctance to baptise Jesus (Matt 3:14). We should be able to generate some sympathy in the listener. Then we describe what happened next. We are telling the story, not just reciting a text, so we can accentuate the unexpectedness of the voice from heaven. John heard it, the crowd heard it.

Next, we ask our listeners whose voice they suppose it was. There is really only one answer, and it may well make them uncomfortable. We can then soften the impact and strengthen the assertion that Jesus is the Son of God by going on to say that although what the voice said was surprising, it reminds us of two other prophets.

God had spoken to David about one of his descendants who would come. God said about him, "I will be his father and he will be my son" (1 Chr 17:11–14). Isaiah was also a great prophet sent to the Jewish people (unknown to Muslims and therefore needing the introduction), and he spoke about the servant of the Lord who would come. Isaiah, who lived seven hundred years before Jesus, speaking the word of God, said, "Here is my servant, whom I uphold, my chosen one in whom I delight; I will put my Spirit on him" (Isa 42:1). On the day Jesus came to John, God drew these two ideas together and applied them to Jesus.

How will our listeners respond? That depends on many things, but we have pointed them to Jesus. If they question his sonship, we can gently ask who God was speaking about when he made that promise to David. If they agree that Jesus is the beloved servant, we can offer to show them what else Isaiah revealed about the "Servant of the Lord."

Whichever direction the conversation takes, our aim is to highlight the uniqueness of Christ and ultimately our need to respond to him. One way of spelling out his uniqueness is to pick up on the link between Jesus and the Holy Spirit. As John said, the one coming after him will baptise with the Spirit. Jesus is the one who brings people into new relationship with God so that they can receive the Holy Spirit. That may lead to an opportunity to share something of the role of the Holy Spirit in your life and the relationship he enables you to have with God.

Opening Up the Scriptures

Yet another way to call on John/Yahya is to ask our Muslim friends if they know about what John said. If they express interest, we can turn to John 1:29–31. This introduces the unfamiliar idea of the Lamb of God. Since it is unfamiliar, it is neutral ground and we should have some curiosity to work with. After all, why would a man be called a lamb? We can, of course, answer this implied question with reference to stories. Moses taught people that they needed to offer sacrifices to be right with God. The people had to sacrifice a lamb just before they were freed from the land of Egypt. God provided a ram to save Abraham's son. All of these pointed forward to a greater sacrifice for all of humanity—the Lamb of God—who takes away the sin of the world.

If our listeners are able to take more in, we might continue down to John 1:34, where John declares Jesus to be (according to most translations—be sure you know what yours uses) the Son of God.

Continuing with the theme of John/Yahya, we read in Luke 7:16–24 about John wondering, while he is in prison, if Jesus is really the one. We are used to thinking about this as John being discouraged and doubting. But for Muslims, the question, "Should we expect someone else?" has an entirely different ring to it. In their mind, the identity of the final prophet is paramount, and it sounds like John is asking if Jesus is the last prophet. And in a way he is. He is asking if the promises and purposes of God are to be fulfilled in Jesus or in someone who was still to come. This may be a story we can use in response to questions such as "Why don't you believe in the last prophet?" Our reply can be based on the words of John and Jesus. John asked if we should expect someone else. Jesus responded by pointing to the things he was doing: his works of healing, the very things promised as signs by the prophets long ago. Has anyone come since doing these things? Even if our Muslim friends don't accept this, they may go away thinking about it carefully because these are the words of one of their prophets.

Calling on Zechariah in Our Witness

Zechariah gives us more to work with than you might think. The strong link that Islam makes between Zechariah and Mary means that a discussion about Zechariah can quickly lead to the Virgin Birth of Christ and his uniqueness.

Zechariah's prophecy (Luke 1:68–79) is mainly about Jesus. He refers to him as a "horn of salvation," which is an awkward phrase but is helpful because it puts the focus on salvation rather than just being a messenger. Zechariah also makes connections with David and Abraham, which enables us to call on them in the ways discussed elsewhere in this book. Zechariah's prophecy speaks of promises and covenants, something not well understood among Muslim people, making them neutral territory. Explaining them gives us a chance to tell the story of salvation and to describe how God is portrayed in the Bible.

Chapter 14 Jesus Christ (Isa al-Maseeh)

Some years ago, I participated in a very well-known family Bible week in the UK. There was always a missions section, and this particular year the leaders decided to create a "mission experience" for the people to pass through. Nice Christian people who had come to have a good time with their families were led through a series of interactive simulations, at the end of which they found themselves confronted by me. I was sitting cross-legged on a mat, dressed like a Muslim teacher, with what looked like a Qur'an on a bookstand in front of me. It was actually an Arabic Bible, but that's not important here.

My task was to engage the participants in some dialogue. It generally went something like this. I would welcome a group of about twenty people and ask them to confirm that they were Christians, which of course they did. Then I asked them, "If you had the choice of drinking fresh milk or drinking milk that was a week old, which would you choose?"

They would warily reply, "The fresh."

I would say, "Of course you would choose the fresh. So you should believe in Muhammad, who came more recently than Jesus."

Many would then respond, "Ah, but you don't believe Jesus is the Son of God, do you?"

"No, of course not," I would reply. "The very idea is scandalous. How can you say such a thing?"

Then they would say, "Well, he is. In fact, he is God."

I would reply that they weren't making any sense. How could God be his own son?

Time and time again, they got into a tangle trying to tell me why Jesus was so much more than a prophet. Many also became angry and even a bit hostile. I would often have to step out of character and try to help them.

Toward the end of the week, an older Afro-Caribbean lady came in with a small group of just three or four people. On hearing my opening gambit about the milk, she looked me in the eye and said, "But Jesus gives us living water."

I was so excited that I had to step out of character and congratulate her. It was such an unexpected and intriguing answer. It opened the way to speak in terms of personal experience or perhaps about what people really need or even to simply tell stories about Jesus. It was beautiful. Most of the others had been defending their faith and ultimately themselves. This lady felt no need to defend anything; she raised the level of the conversation to point to Christ.

The Prophet Jesus?

Many Christians find it difficult to refer to Jesus as a prophet. Isn't the whole point that he is God, the second person of the Trinity, God the Son, and indeed the Son of God—not a mere human prophet? Well, yes, but the very complexity of that statement should make us pause.

Jesus himself accepted the label of prophet (Matt 13:57; Mark 6:4; Luke 4:24; 13:33). In John 9, we see a man born blind working out who Jesus was. At one stage, he affirmed that Jesus was a prophet before he came to a deeper understanding. In Acts 3:22, the apostles did not hesitate to identify Jesus as the *prophet* foretold by Moses.

Let's think about it this way. If you can see your destination a short distance ahead of you, but the most direct route means crossing a raging river, you could just plunge in and fight your way across. You might even make it. On the other hand, it might be worth your while to walk along the bank some distance, find a solid bridge, cross it, and then walk back on the other side to where you wanted to get to. It takes longer, but it is a surer route.

The fact is that Islam has a well-rehearsed narrative about Jesus. We could start by confronting it and rejecting it from the outset, which would be like plunging into the river. On the other hand, we could start where our Muslim friends are, walk with them, and then lead our listeners out of that narrative and beyond it. We want them to know who Jesus is, but we need to start where they are and lead them from there to a suitable bridge. If Muslims affirm Jesus as a mighty prophet, that is a great place to start. Requiring them to swallow the whole theological formula in one mouthful, however, is a huge ask.

Jesus in Islam

The name of Jesus occurs much more frequently in the Qur'an than that of Muhammad. That should not really surprise us in light of Islam's claim that the Qur'an is a collection of words spoken *to* and *through* Muhammad, not *about* him. Muhammad operated in an environment in which Jews spoke proudly of their prophet Moses, while Christians spoke of Jesus as Son of God and as the second member of the Trinity. In his own mind, Muhammad was building on the foundation that God had laid in these other faiths, correcting their departures from the truth and completing them. For this reason, the Qur'an had to speak about Jesus.

The Qur'an gives an account of Jesus' birth in Q 3:42–51 and Q 19:16–35. The birth of Mary and her upbringing are recorded as well, in Q 3:35–37. As we have seen, Islamic tradition supplies names for many anonymous women in the Bible, such as Potiphar's wife and the Queen of Sheba, but the one and only woman to be named in the Qur'an itself is Mary. The Qur'an affirms the Virgin Birth without equivocation, and it has Jesus speaking to people when he was still a newborn baby.

However, Muslims are taught that Jesus was created by God as a special sign and that he should not be regarded as more than human. Here are some statements in the Qur'an that underpin this view: "It is not for God to have a child—glory be to Him. To have anything done, He says to it, 'Be,' and it becomes" (Q 19:35). "The likeness of Jesus in God's sight is that of Adam: He created him from dust, then said to him, 'Be,' and he was" (Q 3:59).

On the basis of these texts, Islamic scholars say that Jesus was created, as Adam was. Although one can see the reasoning, it is clear that Jesus, in the Qur'an, was not created in the same way as Adam, because Adam was created as an adult. Jesus was not only born of a virgin but is marked out as a very special and blessed individual. The Qur'an makes Jesus out to be absolutely unique. His birth is more miraculous than any other, and that should beg some questions.

Much of Islamic teaching actually comes from the vast collection of texts known as the *Hadeeth* literature, which supplies the Qur'an with context by recounting stories and sayings from the life of Muhammad and his immediate companions. There is a very well-known text from the Islamic traditions which says that "Abu Huraira [Muhammad's companion] heard the messenger of God [Muhammad] say: No son of Adam shall be born unless that he should be afflicted (touched) by the Satan at the hour of birth, when he initiates his life crying out of the Satan's touch, except Maryam and her son."[17]

This text is so widely known that I have found references to it on the internet being discussed in terms of whether it accords with scientific knowledge concerning why (and whether) all newborn babies cry. The fact that the text makes such an exceptional claim about Mary and Jesus was just taken as read. Everyone "knows" that the birth of Jesus was extremely special. Nothing of the kind is said about Muhammad.

Nevertheless, it is the custom of most Muslim teachers to emphasise the things which the Qur'an says Jesus is not—not God nor the Son of God—rather than celebrating the extraordinary qualities attributed to him. My point is that what the Qur'an says and what every Muslim "knows" the Qur'an says are often not the same.

The Qur'an repeatedly declares that God has no son and that none is to be worshipped except God alone. This is stated in the strongest terms, for example in Q 19:88–95, but it is generally thought that what is being rejected is the idea that God had some kind of sexual union from which Jesus was produced—which, of course, no Christian believes.

The Qur'an affirms that Jesus performed miracles such as opening the eyes of the blind, making lepers whole, raising the dead, and even performing acts of creation (Q 3:49; 5:110). It refers to Jesus as a sign to humanity (Q 19:21). He is called "a word from God" (Q 3:45), "his word" (Q 4:171), and "the word of truth" (Q 19:34).

Muslim scholars have assigned titles to some of the great prophets and these titles are well known. Abraham is called *Khaleel Allah*, "the friend of God," and Jesus is called *Kalimat Allah*, "the Word of God." That exact phrase doesn't occur in the Qur'an, but that Jesus is *Kalimat Allah* is very well known. A second title given to Jesus is *Ruh Allah*, "the Spirit of God," which is especially common in devotional literature. The Qur'an itself uses the expression "a spirit from Him" (Q 4:171). It is certainly possible to witness to Christ using the Qur'an as a starting point, but that is not the purpose of this book. We are talking about what the Qur'an says here only as useful background information. An approach using the Qur'an is best taken by former Muslims or Christians with a great deal of specialist knowledge.

The Qur'an designates Jesus as the Messiah, *al-Maseeh* (Q 3:45 and ten other places), but the word *Messiah* is treated as a name rather than a rank, title, or function. Neither the Qur'an nor Islamic teachers support the biblical understanding of the word *Messiah*. It is not commonly given any meaning at all.

17 This hadeeth is to be found in two of the most highly rated collections, those of Bukhari and Muslim, and is classed as authentic. Sahih al-Bukhari; 3431. Sahih Muslim, 5837.

The Qur'an makes one clear mention of the crucifixion, in Q 4:157–58:

> And for their saying, "We have killed the Messiah, Jesus, the son of Mary, the Messenger of God," in fact, they did not kill him, nor did they crucify him, but it appeared to them as if they did. Indeed, those who differ about him are in doubt about it. They have no knowledge of it, except the following of assumptions. Certainly, they did not kill him. Rather, God raised him up to Himself. God is Mighty and Wise.

The English translations of "it appeared to them as if they did" vary a good deal. Some translations add that someone was put in his place. This text is taken as the basis for teaching that Jesus was not crucified or killed, but rather God removed him from the scene.

Careful readers of the text, including a small minority of Islamic scholars, recognise that the text is a denial of *someone's claim*, not an actual denial of his death. The "We" here refers to the Jews who, among other things, claimed to have successfully killed Jesus. Since Jesus declared that no one would take his life, but that he freely chose to lay it down (John 10:18), some Christians claim there is no fundamental contradiction here; but the fact remains that despite the various possible interpretations of the verse, Muslims are taught that Jesus was neither killed nor crucified, even though Jews and Christians claim he was. The Muslim story is that God outwitted them and saved his faithful servant Jesus. The exact details vary from one tradition to another. Clearly such a version of events leaves no place for Christ being a willing sacrifice or for his resurrection.

Some Christians go further and say that the Qur'an does acknowledge the death and resurrection of Christ in Q 3:55, where God said,

> O Jesus, I am terminating your life and raising you to Me, and clearing you of those who disbelieve. And I will make those who follow you superior to those who disbelieve, until the Day of Resurrection. Then to Me is your return; then I will judge between you regarding what you were disputing.

The expression "terminating your life" is one of many different translations of the Arabic *mutawaffika*, which, normally speaking, means "causing you to die." Many English translations use phrases like "gathering you up" so that the idea merges with "raising up," but the Arabic definitely refers to a death followed by a raising.

Although this is intriguing, the vast majority of ordinary Muslim people don't find this convincing. In any case, they don't consider themselves competent to interpret the text, and still less that we Christians could be competent to interpret it. Those who come out of Islam and look back often do go to this text and to the ambiguities in the one about the crucifixion to make a case for the Islamic scholars deliberately suppressing the truth despite what Muhammad knew to be true.

The Qur'an makes no explicit mention of the return of Christ, but all Muslims are taught that he will return and slay the Anti-Christ (*Dajjal*) before the end of the world. Many also say he will die and be buried to be resurrected on the last day. Accounts of what will happen at the end of time vary from tradition to tradition, but all of them expect Christ to return.[18] Interest in the end times is currently great, and the signs are much discussed among earnest Muslims.

Here is a basic summary comparing Jesus in Islam with Jesus in Christianity.

Jesus in Islam	Jesus in Christianity
Born of Mary, a virgin	Born of Mary, a virgin
Special creation	God incarnate
As a child, created birds from clay	First miracle as an adult (John 2:11), but childhood miracles present in non-biblical literature
Word of God	Word of God
Spirit of God	Anointed by the Holy Spirit (Luke 4:18; Acts 10:38) and sender of the Holy Spirit (Luke 3:16; Acts 2:33)
Messiah (mere name)	Messiah: God's anointed king, promised by the prophets
Son of Mary	Son of David, Son of Man, Son of God.
Gave sight to the blind	Gave sight to the blind
Cleansed lepers	Cleansed lepers
Raised the dead	Raised the dead
Affirmed the Torah	Affirmed and interpreted the Torah
Rejected by the Jews	Rejected by the Jews
Spared the cross	Betrayed, sentenced, flogged, crucified
Will die and then be raised with everyone else	Raised from death
Alive today, never died	Alive today, having been raised
Located in the heavens	Seated at right hand of God
His return prepares the way for the end	Will return to gather his own and judge the world

18 Except the Ahmadiyya sect, which claims that he has returned already in the form of their founder, Mira Ghulam Ahmad. They are regarded by most Muslims as a heretical sect, not worthy to be called Muslims.

Calling on Jesus in Our Witness

Our witness is to Christ as the Saviour and Lord given by God for all peoples. We can choose to use the words and actions of Jesus in order to direct people toward him rather than arguing for his place in a theological construction. We can refer to the person of Jesus, giving our listeners a reason to ask for more, to read Scripture, and to trust him—or, in other words—to become his disciples (cf. Matt 28:19).

1. The Proverbial Sayings of Jesus

One way of bringing Jesus, "their prophet," into everyday conversation is to quote something he said. This is not about proving anything or preaching; it is about identifying ourselves as followers of Jesus and bringing his word into our interaction. This way of talking may not be familiar in our culture, but Muslims often quote Muhammad, so they will not be surprised when Christians quote Jesus. We are not in the habit of thinking of his teaching in terms of proverbial sayings, but he delivered many pithy statements that we can use and attribute to him. If some are a little cryptic, that is fine. They may give you opportunity to explain more or even to open up the Scriptures to someone.

Here is a brief selection. You can build your own collection.

- Life is not measured by how much you own. Luke 12:15.
- If you love only those who love you, what reward is there for that? Matthew 5:46.
- Why worry about a speck in your friend's eye when you have a log in your own? Matthew 7:3.
- Give to Caesar what is Caesar's. Give to God's what is God's. Luke 20:25.
- Man does not live by bread alone, but by every word that comes from the mouth of God. Matthew 4:4.
- You should say, "We are unworthy servants who have simply done our duty." Luke 17:10.
- Don't worry about tomorrow, for tomorrow will bring its own worries. Today's trouble is enough for today. Matthew 6:34.
- If the blind lead the blind, both will fall into a ditch. Matthew 15:14.
- He who is faithful in a very little is faithful also in much; and he who is dishonest in a very little is dishonest also in much. Luke 16:10.
- By their fruit you will know them. Matthew 7:20.
- Do to others what you would have them do to you. This sums up the Law and the Prophets. Matthew 7:12.

- Out of the fulness of the heart, the mouth speaks. Matthew 12:34.
- Blessed are the merciful, for they shall receive mercy. Matthew 5:7.
- It is more blessed to give than to receive. Acts 20:35.
- He who loves his life will lose it. John 12:25.
- Wide is the gate and broad is the road that leads to destruction, and many enter through it. Matthew 7:13.

2. Stories

People listen to stories and remember them better than statements. The Bible is full of stories. Jesus often responded to a question by telling a story. We would do well to follow his example. Reading from the page is one option,[19] if we know exactly where to find what we need and if we can organise ourselves well; but we can also retell stories about Jesus with greater animation than is possible by simply reading. We can also highlight key points in our telling and fill in background information which might be needed by our listener. Telling stories is a skill we should cultivate.

The Christian tradition of the West has become very used to drawing on the style of statements that we find in the creeds, but the early church set a high value on the narrative content of the Gospels.[20] No particular story will express all that we might want our friend to understand about Christ, but each story fills out a little more about who he is, what he is like, and that salvation is found through faith in him.

What stories might we use? There are many to choose from. Islam teaches that Jesus performed miracles of healing. As we saw above, the Qur'an specifically refers to Jesus healing the blind, cleansing the lepers, and raising the dead. When, for example, a friend is telling us how great the Muslim appreciation of Jesus is and that they know he performed miracles, that is an opportunity to offer to show them an actual story in the Bible or to ask, "Have you heard how Jesus he healed the man born blind?" and to tell the story—or indeed any other appropriate story. As a rule, Muslims only know that Jesus performed miracles, but not the fleshed-out details. With their consent, you create yourself space to speak of Christ.

Here are some accounts of Jesus healing specific individuals. The two stand-out stories of specific individuals receiving their sight are that of Bartimaeus (Mark 10:46–52) and the man born blind (John 9:1–41). In different ways, each

19 If you take the reading option, then note that as a general rule accounts in Mark and Luke give more detail than those in Matthew.

20 See, for example, N. T. Wright, *How God Became King: The Forgotten Story of the Gospel* (New York: HarperCollins, 2016), 18–20.

of these makes reference to the identity of Jesus and results in the healed men acknowledging him. Bartimaeus calls out to Jesus as the "Son of David," which enables us to tap into what that means. With regard to the man born blind, don't miss the fact that Jesus spat and made mud to heal the man. The fact that the *saliva* of Jesus, even combined with unclean dust, had the power to bring healing, will speak volumes to a people sensitive to what is clean and unclean and clearly shows the exceptional holiness of Jesus. A significant part of that story is the man working out who Jesus must be and then meeting him.

While many references are made to Jesus healing people suffering from leprosy, two stories are told in detail. One concerns the ten lepers of whom only one returned to thank him (Luke 17:11–19). The other, told in Matthew 8:1–3, Mark 1:40–42, and Luke 5:12–13, speaks of the leper who fell at Jesus' feet, expressing confidence that Jesus was able to heal him, but showing some hesitation about his willingness. Jesus explicitly spoke of his willingness, stretched out his hand, and touched him. To bring this story to life we need to spell out what it was like for leprosy sufferers: the exclusion, the shame, and the hopelessness. They were not permitted to move freely in public or go to places of public worship. Even by approaching Jesus, the man was breaking the rules. He believed in Jesus. He knew Jesus could heal him, but would he want to? Jesus expressed his willingness in words and also by extending his hand and touching him. Most people feared contamination through touch, but the touch of Jesus brought healing and cleansing.

The Gospels give us three different examples of Jesus raising the dead. Interestingly, all three have particular interest for women.

The raising of Jairus' daughter is found in Matthew 9:18–26, Mark 5:21–43, and Luke 8:40–56. Embedded within these narratives is the story of the woman who suffered constant bleeding. These stories are rich in teaching content: the high-status male leader who openly sought help from Jesus; the woman whose condition excluded her from being in public places approached secretly and then became the centre of attention. That Jesus draws her out into public view and then affirms her instead of rebuking her may come as a welcome surprise to some listeners. Then the news comes that, during the delay, Jairus' daughter has died and it is all over. Jesus told Jairus to believe, and then went on to astonish the family by raising the girl. These stories, full of drama and intriguing detail, promote faith in the person of Jesus.

The raising of the widow's son is only found in Luke 7:11–16. It is a much simpler story. When telling it, we need to point out the nature of the widow's loss: not only the emotional pain of losing her only son, whom she doted on, but also the consequences for her future—being left alone in the world with neither husband nor son. Jesus was moved at her plight. He reached out and touched the bier, which normally would make him ritually unclean. He commanded the dead man to rise, and immediately he sat up and began to talk. Quite an impressive portrait of Jesus!

The third example of Jesus raising the dead is the story of Lazarus in John 11:1–43. I would summarise the early part of the story, in which Jesus delays setting off, and concentrate on the relationship. Lazarus was someone Jesus loved. Jesus had often been the guest of Lazarus and his two sisters. Much of the written narrative focuses on the interaction of Jesus with the two sisters regarding who he is and what he can do. We may have heard the story many times and barely appreciate the human and theological drama of it, but these things will have an impact on a first-time hearer.

Of course, should a Muslim friend mention the miracles of Jesus, another avenue to explore would be the miracles they have *not* heard of. Of these, the encounters with demons are perhaps the most useful. The main two are the man in the synagogue at Capernaum and the man known as Legion.

In the story of the man in the synagogue (Mark 1:21–28 and Luke 4:31–37), the action takes place in an environment much like that of a mosque—a place for prayer and teaching. The accounts link together Jesus' authority to teach and to impose his will on demons. The testimony of the spirit, which after all can perceive things people might not, is also a significant element. Jesus silences but does not contradict him. Concerns around the presence of various kinds of spirit are widespread among Muslim people, even in apparently modern and secular settings. That Jesus drove out demons and gave his followers the authority to do the same is one element of the good news.

The story of the man possessed by so many demons that they called themselves "Legion" (Matt 8:28–34; Mark 5:1–20; Luke 8:26–39) takes place in a very different setting and features a man who was much more obviously demonised. His nakedness, his unnatural strength, his violence, and his residence among the tombs all paint a frightening picture, all the more so where a fear of spirits is a daily fact of life. We should not suppose, however, that this never applies to people living in a more secular setting. In the story, the spirits recognise Jesus as the Son of God and that his presence is a threat to them. Jesus' mastery of the situation is compelling. He not only delivers the man but also commissions him to be his messenger.

One of the most powerful stories to use with a Muslim audience is the healing of the paralysed man (Matt 9:1–8; Mark 2:1–12; Luke 5:17–26). It presents some things that our Muslim friends already know—namely, that Jesus performed miracles of healing and that he knew people's thoughts. It also presents something that they do not know—namely, that he brings forgiveness of sins. In addition, the religious teachers give voice to the orthodox Islamic argument that only God can forgive sins, a thought which Jesus meets head on. Theologically, this is rich material. Furthermore, it is a wonderful and dramatic story full of human interest.

The story of the woman caught in adultery (John 8:1–11) is one we Christians tend to be very fond of. It looks like a good contrast between Christianity and Islam. It is, but not necessarily in the way we expect. It deserves special attention.

This story is a classic example of Jesus giving an indirect answer to a direct question. Westerners tend to read it as Jesus showing grace and forgiveness in contrast to legalism, a triumph of mercy over judgement. We tend to assume that Jesus should side with the woman against the legalists. And we see this picture of grace as attractive. However, we cannot assume that Muslim people, men or women, will necessarily read it this way. The idea that adulterers should be simply "let off" is deeply subversive for them. Even if they happen to be law-breakers themselves (but haven't been caught!), the idea that God's prophet would take the side of the guilty is hard to process. And if we read it carefully, we find that isn't quite what happened. One of the benefits of spending time learning about how Muslims think is that we may start to learn to read some passages with a richer understanding.

Did Jesus pronounce forgiveness? No, that word is never used in this story. He sentenced her to death. The sentence was not carried out because no one was ready to cast the first stone, as Jesus anticipated, of course. He said he did not condemn her, but then a matter was traditionally established by the testimony of two or three witnesses, and all the witnesses had withdrawn. The story is not so much about the woman's guilt as it is about the cynical, inhumane way she was being exposed to shame by a group of insincere men who were only interested in creating problems for Jesus.

Jesus was in a very public place—the temple courts (John 8:2). The woman was caught, we read, in the act of adultery (8:3). So where was the man? If the accusers were concerned with the Law, why weren't they pursuing him? The group of men came and placed the woman in front of the people Jesus was teaching. Knowing full well that Roman law did not permit the Jewish community to carry out an execution under their own law, they put Jesus to the test (8:6). Religious leaders using the laws of God to advance their own agenda won't be unfamiliar to Muslim ears. Even without any sentence being passed, this woman had already been deeply humiliated. How would Jesus react?

Whether Jesus wrote out the law in the dust or whether he was simply avoiding eye contact to protect the woman from further pain, we don't know (8:6–8). By inviting the accusers to present themselves as sinless, and on that basis qualified to carry out the sentence, he turned the tables on them. Now they were on public display—before the watching crowd—their hypocrisy and cynicism were exposed, and so they left the scene.

Finally, Jesus addressed the woman firmly but fairly. He did not condemn her. He did instruct her to change her life—in other words, to repent—and then he let her go. He gave her another chance. He had released her from the power of the men who were using her. And as she went back into the community, she knew that everyone who had accused her had acknowledged their own guilt by backing down.

Jesus emerges from this complex little story as the one who gives the victim a second chance without condoning anything. He shows himself to be the friend of sinners without in any way excusing sin. He also draws out the hidden sinfulness of the religious zealots. It's not that we need to spell all that out for our listeners—after all, Jesus didn't—but we do need to tell the story so as to let it speak to these matters and not gloss it with a simple message that Jesus excuses all sin. That would only tend to confirm the popular perception that Christians have no solid morals.

The examples given above do not exhaust the supply. These are some of the most generally applicable. Once we develop the habit of using these stories, we will find more examples. We need to keep deepening our knowledge of the Gospels. Some stories will speak to very particular circumstances. We need to know them and have thought ahead of time how they can be used.

3. Parables

Jesus often spoke in parables. In our Bibles, some are given the title of parable and others are not. What they have in common is that their message is not explicit. Jesus sometimes told a parable in answer to a direct question (for example, Luke 10:29–37 and Luke 12:41–48). In other words, Jesus chose to give an answer that dealt with the issue in a way that didn't match the thinking of the questioner, nor did he spell out in detail what they needed to know. He was quite at ease being enigmatic, and sometimes we need to do the same.

For example, suppose someone is asking pointed questions because "the gospel does not make sense." There might be a case for stopping them and saying, "Let me tell you something that the prophet Jesus said," and then to relate the parables of the hidden treasure and the pearl of great price (Matt 13:44–46). Then we ask them what they think he meant. We don't correct them; we just leave it with them. If they answer well, we might even give them enigmatic encouragement the way Jesus did in Mark 12:34: "You are not far from the kingdom of God." We don't have to take on ourselves the responsibility of proving everything or even making everything crystal clear. Often people are just not ready.

I once used the "two gates" (Matt 7:13–14) with a friendly Muslim man who was affirming our common ground—suggesting that we are basically the same, we are all on the same path. I neither agreed nor disagreed. I said that I wasn't sure and asked him if I could show him what Jesus said. I then invited him to read the passage. What grabbed his attention was the notion that many were on the road to destruction. We were in a Muslim-majority environment, and this thought shook him.

The parable of the sower (Matt 13:1–9; Mark 4:1–9; Luke 8:1–8) is another example of a parable that we can tell or read and then ask our friends what they think. Jesus went on to give explanations to those who were already disciples, but not to the general public. Bringing the passage into a conversation may shift the focus from who is right and who is wrong to the more significant question of whether we are allowing God to speak to us.

For someone who is keen to say how much Muslims love Jesus, we can ask if they know that Jesus described himself as the Vine. As a rule, this will be unfamiliar. We can then show them John 15:1–17 and invite them as people seeking to take Jesus seriously to say what they understand the passage to say. It covers a lot of unexpected thoughts and holds out mysterious promises and veiled warnings. It puts the emphasis on love, both on our obligation to love and on the love God has for us. If they ask what it means to be joined to Jesus, that is an opportunity for testimony.

For many of us, our favourite parable is the parable of the prodigal son. Maybe compared to a lot of other parables, it seems like a truer representation of the gospel as we are used to thinking of it. If the individuals we are talking to sees themselves as failed Muslims, this parable may have the impact we want it to. They may identify with the wayward son. If they don't see themselves that way, then the story may prove to be an unhelpful puzzle.

4. Answering Standard Muslim Objections

All across the Muslim world, certain lines of argument crop up frequently and predictably. They are part of a well-rehearsed narrative about Islam being right and Christianity being wrong. If we are at all serious about engaging with Muslims, we should be familiar with these standard objections. That doesn't mean we should recite the same memorised answer to everyone. Rather, we should speak to the person who is before us and consider what will be most helpful. People raise the same issues but for different reasons.

For some, it is just what they are supposed to say, but they don't really care. For others, they want to know what the answers are. And for yet others, it is just a verbal sparring match, almost a game. They have no intention of listening.

If we try to respond to someone, and before we have even given our answer they are moving on to another objection, we know that they are not listening. In such a case, we need to change the subject and work on building some common ground and trust. You want to bring the person to the point that they ask an honest question, one that they actually care about.

To address these standard objections and for the purposes of this book, I recommend choosing to use Jesus' own words or an incident in his life and reading that passage directly from the Bible text. For our listeners, authority rests in the person of Jesus, "their prophet," rather than the fact of the words being in a book; but being able to show that it is written means that the dialogue isn't just between us and them. In a sense, we engineer a meeting between Jesus and Scripture on one hand, and our friends on the other. We remain their friend, helping them to make sense of what they are encountering.

The mere fact of offering to take their question seriously and inviting them to read with you acts as a filter. As a rule, those who are just goading or teasing us have no intention of listening to us and are not going to accept the invitation. Those who do accept it, by definition, are more ready to listen and interact.

The aim is not to beat the questioner through argument, but to give them a reason to keep enquiring and to point them to Jesus as Saviour and Lord. I have written more about this approach in my previous book, *Keys: Unlocking the Gospel for Muslims.*

Be careful to work with the objection they raise without straying into a different one. For instance, it is very easy to move unintentionally from Jesus being Son of God to Jesus being God or God being Trinity. Each of these are difficult subjects and become more difficult when muddled together.

Objection 1: "Jesus is not the Son of God"

Why do we make Jesus out to be the Son of God? In reply, we can deny it. I mean, we deny that *we* are the ones making Jesus out to be the Son of God. We turn to Matthew 3:16–17, or one of the other baptism accounts, and show our Muslim friends that a voice spoke from heaven. Whose voice do they think that was. We let them answer. We can then turn to Matthew 17:5 or the other accounts of the Transfiguration. We ask whose voice is speaking. And we ask what the voice commands (that we listen to the Son). With these passages we insist that the title Son of God is not a human invention. We might also suggest that the point is not to argue over the wording but to find out what it means. After all, "God has no wife." This is one of the points Muslims often use to dismiss the idea that God could have a son. With the right build up, we can take that line up ourselves!

Similarly, in Matthew 16:16, Peter declares that Jesus is the Son of God, and Jesus responds that this was revealed by God and did not come from any human source. In Matthew 14:22–32, we see actions speaking louder than words. Jesus is hailed as the Son of God, but without any reference to his birth.

With someone who is really willing to explore, who is already aware of some of the issues, reading John 5:19–27 might be appropriate. Here Jesus speaks of his interaction with God the Father. This also goes beyond titles to talking about what he brings, what his role is, and invites a response.

Objection 2: "Not three but one" (the Trinity)

We should not offer to prove that the Trinity is true, but rather help an enquirer discover it by reading the Scriptures with us. Is the Trinity in the Bible? Yes, it is. In Matthew 28:19–20, Jesus commanded his followers to baptise in the name (singular) of the Father, Son, and Holy Spirit.

Often the objection will come up, without mentioning the Trinity, asking how it is we do not worship the one and only God. In answer to this we can call on the words of Jesus in Matthew 4:10 "Worship the Lord your God, and serve him only." We affirm that as obedient followers of Jesus we do only worship the one true God, but then point out that even the devil knows there is only one God. How is our relationship with that one God? Then we go to Matthew 22:34–38. Jesus says the first and greatest commandment is that we love God with all that we are. Is God worthy of all our love? Of course he is! Are we able to remember God at every instant? Are we able to love him without interruption? If not, we are failing to keep the most important commandment. This moves the conversation on to our need for God's mercy.

Objection 3: "Jesus is not God"

In Luke 20:41–44, Jesus asks the question, "Why is it said that the Messiah is the son of David?" We may need to explain that the Jews understood that the Christ, the Messiah, would be the "Son of David." In this they were quite correct (Matt 1:1), but it was not a sufficient description. Jesus himself quotes David (Psalm 110) to show that David referred to the promised Messiah as his Lord, and so he must be much more than simply his descendant.

In John 8:56–58, we find the culmination of an interaction with Jewish opponents. Jesus uses the phrase 'before Abraham was born, I am. Rather than pressing the point, we can ask what the reader thinks Jesus meant.

In John 14:8–9, we find Philip asking that Jesus show them the Father. Jesus responds that anyone who has seen him has seen the Father.

The book of Revelation contains several declarations made by Jesus. In Revelation 22:12–13, Jesus lays claim to titles normally reserved for God.

Objection 4: "The Bible has been changed"

Jesus speaks to this issue. In Matthew 5:18, he declares that *the text* of the Law of Moses cannot be changed or lost. Then in Matthew 24:35 he declares that heaven and earth will pass away, but his own words will never pass away. This is a more powerful argument in typical Muslim ears than talking about the history of different manuscripts. It also sounds like the sort of thing Jesus ought to say. It has a ring of truth about it to Muslim ears.

Objection 5: "Jesus was not crucified"

This objection concerns not only historical facts but also matters of purpose and meaning. It is important that we don't neglect to talk about the resurrection, as well as the crucifixion, and to describe it as a victory in fulfilment of the will of God, not just something that happened.

Jesus taught that he must be rejected and killed, that this was part of God's sovereign plan. He is recorded as saying so in several places in each of the Gospels. Matthew 16:21–23 is particularly appropriate to use. Peter gives voice to the Muslim objection and is rebutted by Jesus himself.

At the Last Supper (see, for example, Matthew 26:26–29), Jesus talks about his coming death and what it will achieve. He also alludes to life beyond his death. It is another of those passages which we can invite an enquirer to work out for himself or herself what Jesus means.

With someone who wants to explore what the Bible really teaches, we can take any one of the Gospels and carefully read through the words of Jesus on the cross. These serve to show that it was Jesus on the cross, and not, as many Muslims have been told, someone put in his place.

For a bold and clear statement, we can turn to John 10:17–18. Jesus declares that he lays down his life of his own accord. While he does not mention the cross explicitly, the fact that he denies that his death comes about by the mere scheming of people accords unexpectedly with the Qur'anic text that says "They did not kill him," and yet affirms his death.

Jesus spoke of both the fact and purpose of his death in a number of ways. One example is found in John 3:14–15. To make use of this reference, we need to be ready to retell the story of Moses and the bronze snake. After all, people remember stories better than statements. In this passage Jesus states that he will be physically lifted up to be seen, a clear allusion to crucifixion, and spells out the purpose: that those who believe may have eternal life.

Finally—though more references could be called on—in Revelation 1:18, Jesus identifies himself as one who was dead and is alive now and forevermore.

Objection 6: "Jesus foretold the coming of Muhammad, so why do you refuse to believe in him?"

This sounds so simple, but it isn't. To give a flat denial is attacking the Qur'an and Islam, whether or not we intend to do so. By doing so, we shut down the conversation. Muslims are so sure that Jesus did foretell the coming of Muhammad, that in denying it we seem to be showing our ignorance. I find it is best to simply say that we have no reason to believe that Jesus did so and then invite them to show us in the Bible. That keeps an open door.

Some of our friends may have had some training and refer to John 14, the promise that the Comforter will come. There is a popular argument that this refers to Muhammad. If they make this suggestion, one option is to look at the passage with them. It is better for them to find the text and make the claim and then for us to address it with them, than to be the first to raise the possibility that John 14 supports them. We can explore it with them by offering to read all of John 14:15–27 slowly and carefully. It will become abundantly clear that Jesus is not talking about the coming of a prophet. We do not need to get defensive or to tell them they are wrong. If they have genuine questions about what this means, we can turn over a few pages to Acts 1:4–8 (Jesus speaking) and then Acts 2. All of this is giving them exposure to the word of God, and we are positioning ourselves as friends, not combatants.

For your information, Muslim apologists pick out the Greek word translated "comforter" and say that by just changing one letter of one word it becomes "praised one." The literal meaning of the name Muhammad is "praised." They argue that the Greek has been changed just slightly and that when Jesus was foretelling the coming of "another," he meant Muhammad and named him. A careful reading of the passage (rather than just the odd sentence) shows that Jesus could not have been talking about a human being.

Another way of dealing with the issue of why we don't believe in Muhammad is to point out that the time of Jesus has not ended. The Islamic understanding is that each prophet has his time and then another comes along. Jesus himself said he is always with us (Matt 28:20). He needs no successor. This is drawing on a reason that follows Muslim logic and depends on a respectable authority.

If we address this subject in terms of what we don't like about Muhammad, we will be talking about Muhammad, not presenting Christ. We also put our listener into defensive mode, in which he or she will be more concerned to stand their ground than to learn anything new. It is much more appropriate to speak of the many benefits we have in Christ and let our Muslim friend make the comparison for themselves.

5. Words of Jesus Which Are Sweet to the Seeker

There are a number of Jesus' sayings that we would do well to memorise and train ourselves to find in Scripture without difficulty, whenever needed. These are words he spoke to disciples or seekers which have a particularly personal resonance. We want to have these sayings at our fingertips to impart to someone who is really seeking God. We can step in and say, "This is what the Lord Jesus says."

I carry Matthew 11:28–30 on a little card in my wallet at all times ready to give to someone as part of a conversation. It is the "Come to me all you who are weary" text.

I also carry John 14:27: "Peace I leave with you, my peace I give to you." There are many moments when this might be an appropriate quote to use. When I am talking to a Muslim who is very careful to add "Peace be upon him" whenever he mentions Jesus, I start doing the same but with a difference. If they are using the Arabic formula *salaam alayhi,* I start using *salaamahu alayna*. In English that is "May his peace be upon us," which is what I use if they are using the English formula. If they don't pick up on it themselves, I explain that I could never say "Peace be upon him" because it would be inappropriate, maybe even insolent. After all, he is the one who gives peace. What business would I have thinking I could pronounce peace upon him? After all, he himself promised to give peace to us.

Setting aside the use of such formulas, peace is such a rich word representing so much of what people seek. This verse is appropriate in many contexts.

For a seeker who is genuinely considering following Christ, fear is often a major consideration. In Matthew 10:28–31, Jesus speaks both a stern word about not fearing "those who can only kill the body," followed by a comforting word about being "worth more than many sparrows."

Chapter 15 Epilogue—And Finally . . .

On the road to Emmaus, Jesus took the two disciples through the writings of Moses and all the prophets, explaining from all the Scriptures the things concerning himself (Luke 24:27). He was not just speaking of things that had been foretold and had now come true; he was teaching *about himself* and about the role, nature, and purpose of the Christ. In the messages we find recorded in Acts 2, 3, 4, 7, 8, and 13, we find the apostles repeatedly referencing the prophets to support their proclamation that Jesus was the Christ. Later, Paul challenges Agrippa by asking him if he believed the prophets (Acts 26:27). In Acts 15, as the early church wrestled with the issue of accommodating the Gentiles, James drew things together by referring to the words of the prophets.

In Romans, famous for its detailed exposition of the gospel, we find almost a whole chapter about Abraham which also refers briefly to David. Awareness of the story of Moses and the Exodus forms the backdrop of 1 Corinthians 5:6–8 and 10:1–22, while references to Adam are used in chapter 15 of that letter. We started this book making, as it were, a *Muslim* case for calling on the prophets, that the names and voices of the prophets carry a particular resonance for Muslim people. As we bring it to a conclusion, it is good to be reminded that for the apostles themselves referring to the prophets as they proclaimed and explained the good news of Jesus was the norm.

To be sure, there is a difference between their situation and ours. The apostles were speaking to people who were acquainted with the biblical accounts of the prophets. Our Muslim friends have, at one level or another, been told different things about the same prophets and have learned to see them through a different set of lenses. But nevertheless, we are not doing anything novel or strange to make it our practice to regularly draw the prophets into our proclamation of Christ.

Citing the prophets is not the key which unlocks every door. It is something to have in our toolbox along with other things—testimony, answers to difficult questions, stories, the offer of prayer, and so on. To be able to make good use of tools, we need to develop the skill. Skills come through practice. Merely acquiring information will not do it. If you want to learn to the use the prophets, it might help to prepare some exercises and role plays, ideally with an understanding friend. That may sound artificial, but this is how skills are developed. That is how great sports stars perfect their art, by training themselves off the field, as it were.

The aim is that when you are face to face with someone you are trying to communicate with heart to heart, your brain is not working overtime trying to remember something you read in a book. Calling on the prophets becomes second nature through practice. The ideas are familiar, and they flow freely as you give your attention to the person you are talking to and have space to listen to the prompting of the Spirit.

I cannot conclude without coming back to that most fundamental truth that no matter how skilful and knowledgeable we are, without love it counts for nothing (1 Cor 13:1–3). What we do, the way we behave, all kinds of unconscious messages that we impart—these all count for far more than our skills. Who we are will speak louder than what we actually say. Skills and knowledge are good to have, but they are best used by someone who, as Paul puts it, is constrained by the love of Christ and no longer sees anyone from a human point of view (2 Cor 5:14–16). We can trust our living Lord Jesus to teach us and train us.

Appendix 1: Notes on Names

When speaking of the prophets, Muslims will often use the Qur'anic form of the name even when speaking in English. In some areas, these names are further modified in the local language, but are still drawn from the Qur'anic form. An example would be *Da'ooda* in West Africa adapted from *Dawud* (David).

Below is a table of names of prophets found in the Bible and the Quran in their English and Arabic forms for handy reference. The way Arabic names are written in the English alphabet varies considerably in other materials. Here I have used the spelling that I think is the most helpful for accurate pronunciation. For example, a person may write their name as Musa or Moussa, but it is pronounced *Moosa*. Or they might write Ayub, but they say *Ayoob*.

Some persons not discussed in this book are included in the list below. Next to the prophets is a list of women mentioned in the Bible to which Islam ascribes names.

MEN **understood to be prophets in Islam who are also mentioned in the Bible**		**WOMEN** **who are mentioned in prophet stories**	
ARABIC	ENGLISH	ARABIC	ENGLISH
Adam	Adam	Hawwa	Eve
Idrees	Enoch		
Nooh[21]	Noah		
Loot	Lot		
Ibraheem	Abraham	Saara	Sarah
Isma'eel	Ishmael	Haajar	Hagar
Is-haq	Isaac		
Ya'qoob	Jacob		
Yusuf	Joseph	Zuleyka	Wife of Potiphar
Moosa	Moses	Asiya	Wife of Pharaoh
Haaroon	Aaron		
Dawud	David		
Suleimaan	Solomon	Bilqees	Queen of Sheba
Ayoob	Job	Raheema	Wife of Job
Iliyaas	Elijah		
Yoonus	Jonah		
Zakariya	Zechariah		
Yahya	John (the Baptist)		
Isa al-Maseeh	Jesus Christ	Mariyam	Mary

21 The letter *h* is pronounced.

Appendix 2: The Names of Jesus

In the Qur'an and throughout the Muslim world, Jesus is rendered *Isa* (pronounced *Eesa*). However, in the Arab world, most Christians use the form *Yasoo'*. A common claim among the traditional Christian population of the Middle East is that Muhammad changed the name of Jesus from *Yasoo'* to *Isa*. Explanations of why and how this happened vary, but the story is often told with some passion. These Christians go on to say that *Isa* is a false Jesus and *Yasoo'* is the true Jesus. This issue comes up from time to time because it really bothers many Arabic-speaking Christians in the Middle East. Farsi-speaking and Turkish-speaking Christians seem happy enough with *Isa*.

There is, in fact, no evidence to support this claim. While the Qur'an and other Islamic sources are quite bold and explicit about contradicting some Christian teachings, nothing is said anywhere about replacing or "correcting" the name of Jesus. The presence of members of various Christian sects in Arabia in Muhammad's day is well documented. Muhammad intentionally addressed people of Christian allegiance and expected them to recognise the terms he was using, so it is safe to assume that his listeners would be familiar with the use of Isa for Jesus.

In the time of Muhammad, Arabic was not really a written language. It was not a language of education, administration, or Christian worship. In daily life, Christians were speaking a variety of languages used in the region, including Arabic. The languages of worship were Greek and the dialect of Syriac used in Syria. In the early centuries of Islam, some attempts were made by Christians to translate the New Testament into Arabic, and some of them used Isa for Jesus. It didn't seem to be a contentious issue for them in that period.

Our own English version of the name has come to us via a long and tortuous route. The apostles spoke to Jesus and about him in the Aramaic language. They would have said *Yashoo'a*, a common Jewish name that elsewhere we read as "Joshua." When the apostles wrote in Greek, they used the accepted Greek version of Joshua which was *Iesoos*. This was taken into Latin as *Jesus*, with the letter *J* pronounced like a *Y*. At some point, English-speakers started pronouncing the *J* as in "J is for jam." As a result, we now write and say "Jesus" the way we do. In terms of the sounds we use, it is nothing like his original name. French-speakers and German-speakers write his name with the same letters, but they pronounce it differently. Clearly names change as they move from one language to another. In fact, the Irish Gaelic version of Jesus came via Latin, was adjusted to the linguistic requirements of that language, and came out as *Íósa*, pronounced *Eesa*.

However, the meaning of any word is determined by its usage, not by its history. The English word *disaster* originally meant "according to the stars," but now it means "a very bad happening." The stars don't come into it. How we use the word determines what it means. If you ask Muslims anywhere in the world for the name of the person Christians say is the Son of God and was crucified, they will say Isa. Just because they don't have the same beliefs as Christians doesn't mean that we are talking about a different person. If, for whatever reason, we use a different Arabic name for Jesus, they simply won't know who we are talking about.

In my experience, most English-speaking Muslims have no problem using the name Jesus when speaking in English, so as a rule we don't need to worry about this issue. I mention it here because from time to time someone comes along saying that Muhammad changed the name of Jesus, and it has become an issue in their interaction with Muslims.

Other Titles by the Author

Clues to Africa, Islam, and the Gospel: Insights for New Workers

Drawing on decades of engagement in Africa, Colin Bearup has compiled a thoughtful collection of questions, insights, and narratives to guide the reader into a deeper appreciation for the nuances of African Islamic worldviews. A winsome and practical book of hard-won wisdom, *Clues to Africa, Islam, and the Gospel* is destined to become a go-to resource for those working on the continent.

116-page paperback, www.missionbooks.org

Keys: Unlocking the Gospel for Muslims

This is a very practical teach-yourself guide to opening up the gospel for Muslims. It is about giving our Muslim friends exposure to Jesus rather than defeating them in argument. Drawing on forty years of experience, Colin Bearup looks at responding to their questions and objections, telling and applying stories, and reading with them. A good part of the book consists of a guide to reading Matthew's Gospel with a Muslim friend.

168-page paperback, www.amazon.com

Inviting Muslims to Church: How to Plan and Hold a Guest Service for People of Islamic Faith

Based on recent experiences with a British church, this concise and practical guide gives advice on how to hold a guest service especially for Muslim friends and neighbours.

28-page booklet, https://grovebooks.co.uk

Lightning Source UK Ltd.
Milton Keynes UK
UKHW021554120921
390445UK00012B/253